Trump Catalog

Trump Catalog

THOUGHT CATALOG

THOUGHT
CATALOG
Books

BROOKLYN, NY

THOUGHT CATALOG Books

Published by Thought Catalog Books, a division of The Thought & Expression Co., Williamsburg, Brooklyn. Founded in 2010, Thought Catalog is a website and imprint dedicated to your ideas and stories. We publish fiction and non-fiction from emerging and established writers across all genres. For general information and submissions: manuscripts@thoughtcatalog.com.

First edition, 2017

ISBN: 978-1542638296

Printed and bound in the United States.

10 9 8 7 6 5 4 3 2 1

Contents

Part III.

Part V.

PART 1

On June 16th, 2015 Donald J. Trump announced his candidacy for the Presidency of the United States. During that time I had just joined the Thought Catalog staff, and any mention of Trump that came through our submissions inbox were likely to be dismissive and mocking. As the race progressed, our staff wrote and our contributors submitted a variety of articles that accented the choices of the 2016 Election. From deep thinkpieces to examinations of specific issues, personal opinion pieces, and short write-ups about the latest "crazy" thing Donald Trump said, our site became a large catalog of this election and the thoughts people had during it.

In this book, we present, in chronological order, some of the best (or at least most distinctive) pieces on President Donald Trump and his unexpected and unprecedented rise to power. We present them without comment or agenda; this is an honest snapshot of the dialogue we curated over the last year and a half.

—*Jacob Geers*

Donald Trump Wants The Entire World To Know That A Mexican Drug Lord Might Be After Him

Jacob Geers

Donald Trump has telephoned the FBI today after he was "threatened" by the son of escaped drug lord Joaquin "El Chapo" Guzman from a Mexican prison. This was the tweet that Trump is citing as the threat against him:

Sigue chingando y voy hacer que te tragues todas tus putas palabras pinche guero cagaleche @realDonaldTrump

— Joaquín Guzmán Loera (@ElChap0Guzman) July 12, 2015[1]

---

1. *https://twitter.com/ElChap0Guzman/status/620340119896133636*

Rough English translation from TMZ: *"Keep f***ing around and I'm gonna make you swallow your bitch words you f***ing whitey milks***tter (that's a homophobic slur)."*

This tweet comes after Trump threatened El Chapo hours before, saying that he could "kick his ass" (or negotiate with him? It's unclear which).

Donald J. Trump ✔
@realDonaldTrump   ▼ Follow

Can you envision Jeb Bush or Hillary Clinton negotiating with 'El Chapo', the Mexican drug lord who escaped from prison? ....
7:25 PM - 12 Jul 2015

↩   ⟲ 5,348   ♥ 4,382

Donald J. Trump ✔
@realDonaldTrump   ▼ Follow

...Trump, however, would kick his ass!
7:29 PM - 12 Jul 2015

↩   ⟲ 5,423   ♥ 5,401

Trump then uses the prison break as vindication (??) for his bizarre views.

Donald J. Trump ✓
@realDonaldTrump

🐦 Follow

Mexico's biggest drug lord escapes from jail. Unbelievable corruption and USA is paying the price. I told you so!

4:03 PM - 12 Jul 2015

↩ ⟲ 7,121 ♥ 7,970

And asks for a full apology from the media.

Donald J. Trump ✓
@realDonaldTrump

🐦 Follow

When will people, and the media, start to apologize to me for my statement, "Mexico is sending....", which turned out to be true? El Chapo

5:59 AM - 13 Jul 2015

↩ ⟲ 2,200 ♥ 3,553

It's hard to even know where to start with this story, but I think the first thought I have is that a drug lord escaping from prison ≠ Donald Trump being "right" about immigration. Trump's immigration policy basically amounts to believing that emigrating Mexicans are rapists and criminals. You know who are rapists and murderers? Rapists and criminals. And, yes, the law of big numbers suggest that some of them cross the Mexican border in the United States, but there is no statistical evidence anywhere in the world that suggests most illegal immigrants are violent criminals.

But regardless, his immigration argument has absolutely **noth-**

ing to do with El Chapo escaping from prison. We have two things here that are not related:

1. Donald Trump's theory that illegal immigrants are almost all rapists and drug dealers.
2. A really bad crook escapes from jail.

Venn Diagram Displaying The Overlap Between These Two Points

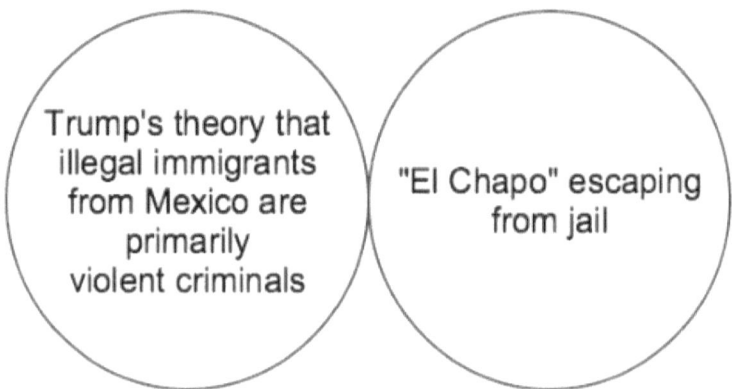

The fact that El Chapo escaped from jail has nothing to do with the border or immigration issues. Trump is asserting that since somebody in Mexico escaped from jail, it proves his stance that most illegal immigrants are violent criminals. It's not even apples and oranges, it's apples and rocks.

This is all yet another demonstration of Trump's magical power to make absolutely *anything* about him. *El Chapo escapes from prison? Oh, that totally vindicates my immigration "stance." Oh, also I bet he is after me! Better tell the FBI, better tell the media!*

And if Trump is honestly fearful for his safety he should call law enforcement. That is totally why they are there. But we all know it isn't about that. It is about trying to headline yet another news cycle with either (1) his bizarre (i.e. false) claims of vindication or (2) typecasting himself as some brave warrior standing up to the drug lords who are "after him."

There is also something to said for **not** tweeting to some drug lord telling them that you will "kick their ass" if you don't want them to tweet back to you.

2

Donald Trump Told Carly Fiorina She Was Too Ugly To Be President, She Gave Him The Response He Deserved

Jacob Geers

Donald Trump has said some pretty awful stuff through the course of his "presidential campaign," but his latest statement about former Hewlett-Packard CEO and presidential candidate Carly Fiorina may mark a new low:

> *"Look at that face! Would anyone vote for that? Can you imagine that, the face of our next president!? I mean, she's a woman, and I'm not s'posedta say bad things, but really,*

folks, come on. Are we serious?"
—**Donald J. Trump**

Trump made this comment about Fiorina after she appeared on a television while he was being interviewed by Rolling Stone magazine.

This is yet another in an endless stream of sexist remarks from Mr. Trump, adding to those that have been directed at Fox News anchor Megyn Kelly and TV personality Rosie O'Donnell:

> *"If I were running The View, I'd fire Rosie. I'd look her right in that fat, ugly face of hers and say, "Rosie, you're fired." We're all a little chubby but Rosie's just worse than most of us. But it's not the chubbiness—Rosie is a very unattractive person, both inside and out."*
> —**Donald J. Trump**

But while Donald Trump has received criticism for his outrageous comments before, this time he got absolutely roasted by Fiorina, who appears to be growing weary of his misogynistic shit.

> *"Leadership is not about how big your position or your title is. It's not about how big your office is; it's not about*

how big your airplane, your helicopter, or your ego is. Leadership is about service."
—Carly Fiorina

Fiorina would go on to say that she doesn't plan on asking for an apology because she sees that the "long line of people asking for him to apologize" isn't getting any shorter, and also because she doesn't give a fly about The Donald. When discussing Trump with voters in New Hampshire, she made it clear that she didn't see Trump as leadership material.

"I think Donald Trump is an entertainer. I think I am a leader."
—Carly Fiorina

The bells of truth ring loud and proud.

3

A Comprehensive Ranking Of The Top 18 Most Insane Things Donald Trump Has Said

Jacob Geers

With all the stupid stuff Donald Trump says, it is hard to parse the regular intensity stupid stuff with the really really stupid stuff. Here at Thought Catalog, however, we are going to attempt to do the deed of providing the world with a comprehensive ranking of the 18 most insane things Donald Trump has ever said. Buckle up.

18. Typical creepy and nonsensical Donald Trump.

"My fingers are long and beautiful, as, it has been well been documented, are various other parts of my body."

17. Donald Trump: protecting America by swindling people on rent.

"I rented [Muammar Qaddafi] a piece of land. He paid me more for one night than the land was worth for two years, and then I didn't let him use the land. That's what we should be doing. I don't want to use the word 'screwed', but I screwed him."

16. Yeah, whatever you say Donald.

"I have a great relationship with the Blacks. I've always had a great relationship with the Blacks."

15. The lady doth protest too much me thinks.

"Sorry losers and haters, but my IQ is one of the highest—and you all know it! Please don't feel so stupid or insecure; it's not your fault."

14. Trump talking about Megyn Kelly during the first debate.

"You could see there was blood coming out of her eyes. Blood coming out of her wherever."

13. Donald Trump being v. creepy.

"You know, it doesn't really matter what [the media] writes as long as you've got a young and beautiful piece of ass."

12. Trump's jokes about banging his daughter are getting kinda weird.

"She does have a very nice figure…if Ivanka weren't my daughter, perhaps I'd be dating her."

11. Not-so-casual sexism.

"If I were running *The View*, I'd fire Rosie. I mean, I'd look her right in that fat, ugly face of hers, I'd say, 'Rosie, you're fired.' We're all a little chubby, but Rosie's just worse than most of us."

10. More sexism.

"Arianna Huffington is unattractive both inside and out. I fully understand why her former husband left her for a man- he made a good decision."

9. Donald Trump as a "birther."

"Why doesn't he show his birth certificate? There's something on that birth certificate that he doesn't like."

8. His "explanation" of why he opposes gay marriage.

"It's like in golf. A lot of people—I don't want this to sound trivial—but a lot of people are switching to these really long putters, very unattractive. It's weird. You see these great players with these really long putters, because they can't sink three-footers anymore. And, I hate it. I am a traditionalist. I have so many fabulous friends who happen to be gay, but I am a traditionalist."

7. Trump should burn science textbooks with that Senator who carried a snowball onto the Senate floor.

"It's freezing and snowing in New York. We need global warming!"

6. You probably know this one.

"When Mexico sends its people, they're not sending their best. They're sending people that have lots of problems, and they're bringing those problems to us. They're bringing drugs. They're bringing crime. They're rapists. And some, I assume, are good people."

5. Yup, still more sexism.

"Look at that face! Would anyone vote for that? Can you imagine that, the face of our next president?! […] I mean, she's a woman, and I'm not s'posedta say bad things, but really, folks, come on. Are we serious?"

4. Oh, now The Donald is also an anti-vaxxer.

"I am being proven right about massive vaccinations—the doctors lied. Save our children and their future."

3. That time he gave our a Senator's personal phone number on live TV.

"Let's try it. 202-228-0292. I don't know, it's three or four years ago. Maybe it's an old number."

2. Donald Trump actually characterizing mass-shooters as "geniuses."

"Because you have sick people. [Mass-Shooters] happen to be intelligent. And, you know, they can be sick as hell and they're geniuses in a certain way."

1. Donald Trump thinks McCain is a big loser for being captured.

"He's not a war hero. He's a war hero because he was captured. I like people that weren't captured."

4

What Do Young Adults Think Of Donald Trump? A Dialogue Between A Supporter And A Critic

Kovie Biakolo

As America's election year gets underway with the primaries, arguably the most talked-about and unexpected candidate seeking a nomination is the ever-divisive Donald Trump. Many would label him racist and sexist among many other negative adjectives, while some simply think of him as, "no-nonsense" and someone who refuses to be "politically correct." He has been called a much-needed breath of fresh air to certain sections of society who perceive themselves as forgotten, even newly disenfranchised. While other sections of society might say he has, "the white supremacist vote." But what about young people? Below is a dialogue between two young adults, one who supports Trump, and the other who finds him and his views abhorrent.

Thought Catalog: *Hi all. Firstly, can you tell us a little about yourselves? Secondly, in a few sentences can you sum up your views on Donald Trump?*

Shaun Scott: I'm a Seattle-based writer and filmmaker. I wrote a book for Thought Catalog in 2015 called *Something Better: Millennials and Late Capitalism at the Movies*. I'm currently working on a book called *Millennials and the Moments that Made US: A Cultural History of the U.S. from 1984-present*. I think Donald Trump is a savvy marketer who is not above using racist demagoguery to exacerbate class divisions and bolster his (non-existent) credentials to be President of the United States.

Jeremy Ely: I live in Los Angeles and like to write short stories and have political conversations. I don't really align to the left or to the right, for example, I think Bernie Sanders is awesome, but I also think Donald Trump presents great ideas and that he'd be a great leader for the country. I think the tremendous hatred I see toward him is a little over the top, and his ideas are not as extreme as we make them out to be.

TC: *Trump has been called a racist, sexist, and a whole host of other "-ists." Do you believe this is true, and why or why not?*

JE: I don't find the terms "racist," or "sexist," that powerful anymore, because of how loosely people in our generation will toss these labels on things they don't like. Prior to the Civil Rights Movement, we saw awful racism in this country. Before women could vote, we saw genuine sexism. Now we have a black president and incredible gender equality. Of course, it is not 100% equal, because men are not women, and women are not men. There will never be a pure absolute lack of racism and an absolute lack of gender inequality. The things Trump says, meanwhile, are not actually racist. They're just opinions that are not considered politically correct because of the hypersensitive age we live in.

SS: Donald Trump's credentials as a racist, a classist, and a xenophobe extend far beyond what he says; we should also pay attention to his actions. He was sued by no less than the Department of Justice[1] for discriminatory practices in real estate. His words have led directly to violence against immigrants and people of color[2]. He has argued that the wages of members of the middle class are "too high."[3] As loud as he is, his actions actually speak louder than his words.

TC: *What, in your own words, does it mean to support Donald Trump, given his positioning by different groups as different things? And as one of you is pro-Trump and the other is anti-Trump, what questions do you have of each other?*

SS: Jeremy will have to answer how he feels about supporting a candidate who thinks his wages are too high, and who makes inflammatory statements about immigrants in public while hiring them in private.[4]

JE: I think it's refreshing to have a presidential candidate who

---

1. http://www.dailydot.com/opinion/donald-trump-latino-vote-race-problem/
2. https://www.washingtonpost.com/opinions/mr-trumps-politics-of-incitement/2015/08/21/c33d0f2e-483d-11e5-8ab4-c73967a143d3_story.html
3. http://www.huffingtonpost.com/entry/bernie-sanders-donald-trump-minimum-wage_us_56afcc13e4b0b8d7c2303e12
4. http://www.dailydot.com/opinion/donald-trump-latino-vote-race-problem/

fearlessly states his beliefs, and doesn't buy into the generic "mumbo jumbo" that most politicians preach. Again, I don't think his comments against illegal immigrants classify as racist. Part of the reason American Health Care is such a mess, for example, is because so many people are pouring into this country and it's difficult to classify who is a citizen. And, even if he were racist, he employs thousands of them and gives them a living, and that's very valuable.

SS: Jeremy, what is your evidence for the claim that "health care is a mess" because of immigrants? Concrete data[5] points in the exact opposite direction of what you say; if it weren't for the labor of immigrant communities, many in this country would go without care. And, once and for all, fearlessly stating one's belief does not, in and of itself, make one an eligible candidate to be president; if that were the case, we could elect Beavis or Butthead.

JE: European countries provide health care to all. I think people of all classes should be able to receive health care to keep living; we need to become like Europe. Poor people facing hundreds of thousands of dollars in health bills is not just, or American—all people have the right to a doctor. But if thousands of undocumented people are coming into a country per day, it'll be impossible to institute that policy because who is an American? "The Wall" would solve that.

SS: If you want American health care to resemble European welfare states, I believe you should be backing Bernie Sanders. The "thousands of undocumented people" you talk about are being employed by the candidate you support; he does not

5. http://www.immigrationpolicy.org/sites/default/files/docs/Critical_Care.pdf

have an interest in actually keeping them out, so you shouldn't either. I agree with what you say about access to healthcare being a universal right.

TC: *Moving away from immigration, how do you think Trump does on the world stage? How do you think the international community perceives Trump, and how would they perceive the United States were he to be elected? Would America be viewed as courageous or crazy, and does it matter?*

JE: Firstly, I think it does not matter very much. In life at any level, I think it's valuable to state your beliefs and not be overly concerned with other peoples' perceptions of them. Not to compare Trump to either guy, but Galileo was hated, and Hitler was loved. I'm sure people would think he's crazy, as many do in America, but that's irrelevant because I think he's right: someone needs to be courageous in the face of growing Islamic terrorism and anti-Americanism.

SS: We already know the answer to this question. Several world leaders have denounced Donald Trump, including the Prime Minister of Britain[6]. A petition to ban Trump from traveling to England garnered 600,000 signatures. Recently, a Russian photojournalist traveling in Iowa during the caucus said that Trump reminds him of the megalomania of Putin[7], who is not looked on favorably in the global community. On top of that, several Pentagon staffers (and other government officials) have said they will retire[8] if Trump wins. Trump cannot "make

6. http://www.cnn.com/2015/12/11/politics/donald-trump-world-allies-turn-on-candidate/
7. http://foreignpolicy.com/2016/02/02/a-russian-reporter-goes-to-a-trump-rally-and-feels-at-home/
8. http://www.thedailybeast.com/articles/2015/12/16/pentagon-troops-it-s-us-or-trump.html

America great again" if his election is seen as a national embarrassment. He can't "be courageous in the face of Islamic terrorism" if he's been denounced by Benjamin Netanyahu.

JE: European countries not supporting our president aren't going to have a real effect, I don't think. They hardly do anything for us anyway. If England wants to ban him, that's not our problem, and let's be cognizant of how Putin, the leader of another superpower, actually endorsed him, a potential American leader, which hasn't happened for decades. So I think he can get along with leaders when it matters. Trump has repeatedly said that he will make the military a priority: "I will make our military so strong, we'll never have to use it." I think that's a good state of mind.

TC: *It's a pretty big statement to say, "[European countries] do hardly anything for us anyway." Economic partnerships, political agreements, and support from the international community is important in today's increasingly globalized world, as they always have been since the emergence of the nation-state. With that said, would the election of Trump see a new age of isolationism in the United States? And with trying to fight terrorism, which is a global problem, how does this affect American national security?*

SS: Here's the thing about national security interests; there are no do-overs. Trump is used to filing for bankruptcy when a business venture goes under. Businesses he's owned have done it four times. But four similar errors in judgment will result in the loss of lives. That's not a risk we can afford to take.

JE: As a man who has amassed billions of dollars of wealth working with people, I have confidence that the guy knows how to get along with people when it matters. By "poor judgment"—pissing off the British leader, or Megyn Kelly, when he's just a candidate—isn't going to result in lost lives. Out of the many businesses he's launched, it's only natural that some of them fail. Let's keep in mind that unlike Hillary Clinton, Trump spoke out against the war in Iraq in 2004[9], which has proven to be a disaster and a tragic loss of American and Iraqi lives and money.

SS: Actually, his lapses in judgment have resulted in violence. There was a beating of a Hispanic man[10] in Boston that was tied to his rhetoric. The claim that he will "get along with people when it matters" implies that he has not done so thus far. If it "does not matter" during his bid to be president, it will never matter. He's unfit to lead.

JE: I think his judgment internationally trumps other candidates. In fighting ISIS, for example, Trump has repeatedly called for "taking the oil." That oil now funds ISIS.[11] Other leaders don't have the courage to pitch an idea like this.

SS: Even a broken clock is right two times a day.

TC: *Wrapping this up, all signs point to the likelihood that Trump will not become the next president of the United States. But what, if anything, does it say about the country in 2016, that Trump has managed to galvanize the support he has?*

---

9. http://www.nytimes.com/live/republican-debate-election-2016-cleveland/in-fact-trump-opposed-iraq-war-but-after-it-started
10. https://www.washingtonpost.com/opinions/mr-trumps-politics-of-incitement/2015/08/21/c33d0f2e-483d-11e5-8ab4-c73967a143d3_story.html
11. http://dailycaller.com/2015/11/12/trump-doubles-down-on-wild-idea-about-iraqi-oil/

JE: I hope people focus less on the occasional crazy things he says and keep in mind his rational ideas. He has called for reducing taxes for the lower and middle class, while also taxing people like himself more.[12] I also respect his plan to help the homeless[13]—American homelessness is shameful. I think the support he's got speaks amazingly well to the idea that people will resonate with a person who speaks their language. I think it's his unique, conversational, often humorous tone in speeches is what gets people to truly support him.

SS: All of Trump's (few) progressive ideas are available in other candidates. These other candidates do not come with the added baggage of hate speech that further divides the country and alienates world leaders. Trump represents the cultural triumph of reality television; fortunately, he will not be representing the country as an elected official.

12. http://www.cnn.com/2015/09/28/politics/donald-trump-tax-plan/
13. http://www.mediaite.com/online/trump-some-gopers-would-see-a-person-dying-outside-a-hospital-and-say-let-em-die/

5

Elections 2016: Dear America, Is This The Best You Can Do?

Kovie Biakolo

I moved to the United States in the fall of 2007 for university. In the first few days, upon arriving on campus, there were volunteers asking students if we had registered to vote. My response, "Sorry. I can't. I'm foreign." In the last eight and a half years, that has been my response to many political and official questions, and for many reasons.

Prior to coming to the United States, I had always taken an interest in American history and political systems. In secondary (high) school, part of my concentration in history class was 20th-century America. In university, I would secondarily study politics (political theory) which largely focused on American political systems. America, in my foreign eyes, has always been an enigma. Eight and a half years later, this is still true.

But when I arrived, something exciting was in the air. Or rather someone: Barack Hussein Obama.

It would be disingenuous to say that I wasn't apprehensive. Even as a late teen (as is true in adulthood), I disagreed with Obama on some fundamental issues. Before I continue, a preface is needed: I am a third culture kid—born in Nigeria, raised away from it; with family spread mostly in three continents: Africa, Europe, North America; my parents are highly educated people; my father was a political journalist insisting on democracy during Abacha's Nigeria—a dictatorship. We left Nigeria largely for this reason. My home was political, as it was religious, although the former is something that might have escaped the ordinary observer.

Sill, Obama was interesting. The thought of being here—in the United States—during the time of the first black president was exciting. The idea of a black president in America was something even as children we thought of as unrealistic. I recall times in childhood when amongst my classmates, we would say something was as unlikely to happen as, "America having a black president." But there I was, somewhere between adolescence and adulthood, and it was happening. It can be difficult to remember, but things really do change.

America, in my foreign eyes, has always been an enigma.

I had grown up with a certain view of the world, and with it came disagreement on being either left or right in America's political system. Add to that a suspicion, if not an entire distrust of politicians and government. I have lived in better governments than the one I was born into, but I maintain my apprehension of people who wish to rule over others. Certainly, it is a difficult job, and a thankless one, to be a leader of a country. But one cannot desire the good that comes with it, without also noting the potential evil that comes with it, and power, and the corruption of power, are the greatest of these potential evils.

For what my foreign words are worth, if anything, I believe that President Obama, for all my fundamental disagreements, both in views that he holds and in those held as a consequence of the policies of the office he occupies, has been a good president. History, I think, will be more than kind, and he may even one day be perceived as a *great* president.

However, I have mostly lived in the United States only under Obama, and so perhaps for that and other reasons, I may be biased. But when I regard the potential candidates that may replace Obama, I notice too that there is something in the air. But it's not the excitement or apprehension which I witnessed the year before Obama was elected. Instead, I think, it is a closely related but distinctive feeling: anxiety.

I am weary of this year's elections.

Realistically, one of the following people might be president: Donald Trump, Ted Cruz, Hillary Clinton, and Bernie Sanders. Save for Sanders, when I consider the list of potential presidents, I am thoroughly uninspired. And while I find Sanders a breath of fresh air in many respects, his lack of experience in foreign policy does not inspire confidence. One could make an argument that with the structure of Congress and its current unproductive state, as well as the oligarchy[1] that has overtaken the American political system, and for that matter our economic institutions, a president's real power is manifested mainly in foreign policy decisions and judgments. Again, one could argue.

In Donald Trump, aside from his racism, sexism, Islamophobia, etc., we have an utterly politically incompetent and largely overrated businessman who plays to the emotions of those who wish to "make America great again," and who draw on a fictional memory of the nation, as if there were a time in history or the present when the country wasn't particularly great for straight, white men. In Ted Cruz, we have an overzealous and very likely trigger-happy politician who lacks common sense in rhetoric, and charisma in presentation—both of which are greatly needed presidential attributes. In Hillary Clinton, we have an established politician, whose experience is both her blessing and her curse, as she is viewed even by those who deem her competent, as ultimately untrustworthy. And in Sanders, we have an idealist, who unlike JFK, may be one with some illusions as to the political and economic forces that stand in the way of his potential revolution. (President Kennedy is once quoted as having said, "I am an idealist without illusions.")

When I arrived in 2007, I did not know that 2008 would be a historic year. But hope and change were the words that would come to define it. No words or phrases have come to define this year for Americans. At least, not yet. But as a foreigner, I have already found my own word: weary. I am weary of this year's elections.

1. https://www.youtube.com/watch?v=hDsPWmioSHg

If the voting process is one that is about choosing the lesser of several evils, then I can without any direct political consequence (I'm foreign, I can't vote remember?), claim that Sanders is for many reasons, from where I stand, the candidate that would do the most good, and the least evil. Even though admittedly, he's the long shot of the four. But crazier things have happened—like the election of a black man to the American presidency, with the name *Barack Hussein Obama*.

In the final analysis, and notwithstanding Sanders, when I look at the short list in all its entirety of potential candidates to replace Obama, like The New York Times columnist David Brooks (of all people) has already expressed[2], I know I'm going to miss the current president. But mostly, I look at this list and can't help but think, "Is this the best we can do?"

Though a plain "yes" or "no" might suffice in answering that question, instead I am reminded of an old George Carlin skit[3] in which he says he doesn't complain about politicians because they are simply the product and the reflection of the American public. Ouch. But if old Carlin was right, we have two options: To accept, like Carlin, that this is the best we can do, and to render all complaints about politicians a waste of time and energy. Or we, even those of us who are not citizens, act upon the realization that as a public, we have much work to do before November 2016, and beyond it.

2. http://www.nytimes.com/2016/02/09/opinion/i-miss-barack-obama.html?_r=0
3. https://www.youtube.com/watch?v=07w9K2XR3f0

6

I'm A Mexican Millennial And I'm Voting For Trump

Matt Powers

The Sherlock Holmeses out there might've already spotted an incongruency in that my last name is Powers. If you're good, you've already deduced my father isn't Mexican, and if you're really good, you've deduced I'm half-Irish, leaving me in a unique middle ground regarding the tiresome insistence that identity politics operate as the fulcrum of political affiliation.

My grandpa and his 10 siblings are first-generation Americans who grew up dirt-poor on a farm in Torrance, California. His parents came from Mexico legally. Half of them went to college, two of them served in law enforcement, two of them are multi-millionaires, and my grandpa is a retired aerospace engineer who spent his career with the United States Air Force and still tutors math at a local elementary school in Sacramento, California at the age of 82.

Our family has been to Mexico and back more times than I can count. When I was 15 we helped build, fund, and donate a library, computer lab, and ambulance to a rural village on the outskirts of Culiacan; his parents' birthplace. They always remember their roots, but they're eternally grateful and proud Americans above all else. It might surprise you, but Mexican immigrants who came here legally aren't fans of illegal immigration.

Fast-forward to 2008, my senior year of high school, helping my neighbor and their family load his furniture into a moving truck because he refinanced his mortgage so many times he had nothing left.

Fast-forward to me in 2012, a business major in my senior year of college, applying to more unpaid internships and staring despondently at my computer screen at the Occupy Wall Street movement and wondering how my generation could possibly prosper in a broken system with corrupt politicians who watched us scream from the inside of a burning building only to tell us, "Don't worry, everything will be OK."

Much like the Baby Boomers, anti-American sentiment was and is strong with millennials, but unlike the Baby Boomers, it's justified. Our parents had their Summer of Love acid tab melt on their tongue and passed a joint around a fire pit while the country sold the next generation down the river, but once they woke up hung over on Haight and Ashbury and the regret sunk in, they picked up the newspaper and called handful of companies and walked into a cushy job, started a family, and the "lazy millennial" meme spews from their hypocritical lips.

Identity politics and the excessively nuanced and abstract civil rights movements are the millennial's acid tab; this insistence that what matters above all else is whether or not you support gay marriage, feminism, Black Lives Matter, abortion, and legalized fucking marijuana. If you don't, you're a bigot and here come a handful of phobia-suffixed words from a George Soros-funded "activist"[1] to shame you off of Facebook and back onto Craigslist to look for another unpaid internship.

Call me a conspiracy theorist, but doesn't this never-ending "progressivism" feel a bit like an elaborate ruse? That maybe these issues are meant to keep us divided along the thinnest lines so we can't collectively agree on something? For fuck's sake, I'll argue identity politics all you want, but before I do I'd prefer a sense of financial optimism and the prospect of starting a family before I'm 40.

Enter Donald Trump; a self-funded billionaire swooping down on the political landscape like Batman and demolishing the corporate media like Bane. The man who wrote *The Art of the Deal* wants to renegotiate America's deals in our best interest instead of Bernie's government-enforced wage manipulation that's unsound to anyone who's taken Econ 101.

For decades we've watched these mannequin politicians, shells of human beings, tell us what we wanted to hear, only to leave us with the uncomfortable feeling that they had no control in the matter, and the political establishment has the gall to give us another Bush and Clinton.

---

1. http://www.washingtontimes.com/news/2015/jan/14/george-soros-funds-ferguson-protests-hopes-to-spur/?page=all

The corporate media and self-righteous "progressives" have called Trump racist, sexist, xenophobic, the Antichrist, and Hitler to no avail, his poll numbers keep rising, even with Hispanics. He's scorched the brush of neo-Orwellian political correctness with a flamethrower so we can all finally gather beneath the only identity politics that matter—American ones.

"How could you support Trump, you're Mexican…isn't it time for a female president, you're not a misogynist, are you?" These "progressives" that divide us and foist an identity and political affiliation upon us are the true bigots; with their emotionally charged rhetoric the politicians and media thought they could blind us and redirect us like a stimulus response, but they can't, and they're afraid. And like Thomas Jefferson said, "When the government fears the people, there is liberty."

PART 2

It is now late February and while narrowing losing the Iowa caucuses to Texas Senator Ted Cruz, Donald Trump emerged victorious from the subsequent contests in New Hampshire, South Carolina, and Nevada.

His string of victories has made Trump the frontrunner, however he isn't without rivals. A large contingent of the GOP still proclaims #NeverTrump, with many Republicans calmly reassuring themselves that one the field narrows, Trump will be defeated by one of his remaining opponents.

Over the past few months, Donald Trump-related articles on Thought Catalog have gotten more serious. No longer is he merely the subject of sassy write-ups, people are writing more thoughtful articles about why they do or do not support him.

7

Someone Discovered Donald Trump's Old Blog And What It Says About Him Is Extraordinary

Daniel Hayes

Much has been said about Trump's former Democratic leanings, but posts from his now-defunct Trump University blog reveal exactly how much he's changed.

1. On Gay Marriage

Elton John's Wedding
Posted: 12/22/2005 5:50:00 PM

by **Donald J. Trump**
Chairman, Trump University

There's a lot to celebrate this holiday season. Elton John married his long-time partner David Furnish on December 21. That's the first day that civil partnerships between gay couples became legal in England under the new Civil Partnership Act.

Elton credits David with helping him kick drug and alcohol additions that nearly killed him. The pair has been together for 12 years. I know both of them and they get along wonderfully. It's a marriage that's going to work.

Elton made the ceremony a small private affair involving only his and David's parents as witnesses. The couple just didn't want to make a big deal out of the wedding. They really wanted to keep things low key.

By all accounts, Elton and David had every tabloid and every entertainment magazine knocking at their door begging for exclusive rights to the affair. By some news reports, the couple turned down an offer of $11 million to record their wedding for British television. But Elton said, "Our relationship isn't up for grabs. It doesn't come with a price tag."

In any event, I'm very happy for them. If two people dig each other, they dig each other. Good luck, Elton. Good luck, David. ave a great life.

(But because I wasn't invited, do I still have to send them a toaster?)[1]

Trump now strongly opposes[2] the Supreme Court's decision allowing same-sex marriage.

2. On Corporate Corruption

Corporate Corruption: If You Have to Lie, Cheat, and Steal, You're Just Not Doing it Right
Posted: 8/10/2005 3:46:00 PM
by **Donald J. Trump**
Chairman, Trump University

Recently former Tyco CEO Dennis Kozlowski was con-victed for stealing hundreds of millions of dollars from the company. It was his second go-round in court–the first one ended in a mistrial. You may remember Mr. Kozlowski from the original trial. A video of his lavish party on an Italian island, allegedly paid for with company funds, was last year's high profile corporate scandal. The retrial was a more low-key affair, but it served to remind us of how

1. https://web.archive.org/web/20060507020036/http://donaldtrump.trumpuniversity.com/default.asp?item=121537
2. http://www.hrc.org/2016RepublicanFacts/donald-trump

much business corruption there has been over the past few years.

The people at the forefront of these squalid affairs give business a bad name. Maybe they're greedy, maybe they're "ethically challenged," but ultimately they're incompetent. If you have to lie, cheat, and steal, you're just not doing it right. My career is a model of tough, fair dealing and fantastic success—without shortcuts, without breaking the law.

Back to that video for a moment: For a couple weeks it was all over the news, so most people saw at least a snippet of this cinematic atrocity, including a giddy, red-faced Kozlowski dancing amid ice sculptures and costumed models posing as ancient Roman courtiers.

As I watched this public embarrassment over and over again, it made me realize that my biggest problem with Kozlowski wasn't the alleged corruption, but the lack of taste. The kind of buffoonery associated with this brand of corporate corruption is just distasteful and alien to me. While watching these high-level company officers cavorting on the shareholder's dime, it occurred to me that maybe tackiness is at the heart of corporate corruption.

Like I said, these people give business a bad name. They've served to associate it with scandal, untrustworthiness, greed, and bad taste. But, as I prove everyday, it doesn't have to be that way at all.[3]

Unclear if this opinion has changed but Donald has never shied away from sketchy arm twisting[4] to get what he wanted.

3. On Gender Equality In The Workplace

The first post is by someone who worked for Trump. The second is by Trump himself.

Women at Work
Posted: 10/3/2005 11:45:00 AM
by **Donald J. Trump**
Chairman, Trump University

Often I'm asked whether I think there is a glass ceiling for women in the corporate world. I admit that in many offices that obstacle may still be in place, but I like to think there isn't one in the Trump Organization.

There are several high-ranking women in my organization. Anyone who has watched The Apprentice is familiar with Carolyn Kepcher, who is an executive vice president as well as general manager and chief operating officer for two Trump National golf clubs. She's very smart, very shrewd, and tough as nails. Those are qualities I admire in someone, male or female.

---

3. *https://web.archive.org/web/20060507011550/http://donaldtrump.trumpuniversity.com/ default.asp?item=93588*
4. http://money.cnn.com/2016/03/28/news/trump-apartment-tenants/index.html

Early in the first season of The Apprentice, I warned the female contestants that they were relying too heavily on their sex appeal to win the tasks. I think women have a tough situation in the workplace because of the sexual undertones. The business environment is so cutthroat that men and women learn to use whatever they can to get ahead, including their sexuality. Yet, when women do this, the perception of them changes. That's why women have to work harder to overcome obstacles.

I expect my employees to work long hours and to be available whenever I need them. Sometimes these expectations are more difficult for women to meet than men because they often have more family obligations than men do. I think sometimes this is where the obstacles come into play. It's not that the opportunities aren't there. It's just hat the priorities can be different. Men are often more willing to put their jobs before their families–and I don't think that's a good thing. Women usually will put their families first, or at least give them equal time. The families win, but often that's why women perceive a glass ceiling looming overhead.[5]

Toppling the Ladder of Gender Differences
Posted: 10/7/2005 4:22:00 PM
by **Karen Kahn Wilson.**
Trump University Faculty

---

5. *https://web.archive.org/web/20060507011841/http://donaldtrump.trumpuniversity.com/ default.asp?item=103779*

Recent scientific studies suggest that men's and women's brains are structured in some fundamentally different ways. This new data showing that men and women possess different neurological "hard wiring" indicate that men and women may also approach life–their work and relationships–differently. If these gender differences are aligned with the appropriate business and educational practices, society can optimize the talents of both genders.

Given the positive potential of such revelations, I was confused by two recent experiences. The other day I sent an e-mail to a prominent author whose new book fascinated me. I thought his concepts for new business paradigms might have an interesting impact on the future for both genders in the work place. He thanked me for my note, but said that he didn't want to comment on my questions about men, women, and the workplace because the topic was a "slippery slope."

Several days later, in a meeting with the CEO of a major financial services firm, I mentioned the new studies. I offered my opinion that these ideas suggested new ways to optimize human capital. He became uncomfortable and said that he "didn't feel ready" to explore such a topic even though he acknowledged that I was introducing him to "thought- provoking" ideas.

It is interesting to me that the mere mention of male/female differences, even considering that exploring those *differences might have a positive impact on society, makes people anxious. Our culture translates the word "differences" to mean "better than/worse than" and becomes tied up by the fear of being accused of discrimination. The business community as well as society at large must confront this worldview and transform it into a value-free, horizontal way of considering differences among us.*

Peering under our cranial hoods has yielded some evidence about gender differences. This knowledge, combined with new business practices, has the potential to advance the development of strong, collaborative gender relationships, capable of succeeding in the fast paced, global economy we live in. It will also promote a work culture that can help both men and women maximize their potential.[6]

He's remained relatively consistent on this one. In his book "Crippled America" he says the following[7] about putting a "33-year-old" woman in charge of building Trump Tower in 1983:

None of the people who whine about the way I talk to women mention the fact that I voluntarily promoted gender equality in a male-dominated industry. The women who work and have worked for me will vouch for the fact

6. *https://web.archive.org/web/20060507023008/http://donaldtrump.trumpuniversity.com/default.asp?item=104314*
7. http://quote.ms/1oqdogW

that I was as demanding of them as I was of their male counterparts.

4. The Housing Bubble

The Housing Bubble: Doom and Gloom Don't Pay
Posted: 9/2/2005 2:43:00 PM
by **Donald J. Trump**
Chairman, Trump University

With housing prices continuing to rise into the far reaches of the stratosphere, there's a lot of talk about a housing bubble on the brink of bursting. Scared at the possibility, industry watchers have been preaching impending doom, warning house shoppers to be wary of the real estate market.

As long as interest rates stay low and the dollar stays weak–which is an unfortunate situation, but it happens to be good for real estate–then there will be no burst in the current housing bubble. If interest rates go up precipitously and the dollar gets stronger, then there will be some reduction in housing prices.

How you react to the so-called housing bubble can be a barometer of your business personality. Are you the type of person who takes advantage of positive situations when they present themselves, riding them out as long as they last? Or do you heed every message of doom and gloom, avoiding risks that could be some remarkable opportunities?

Obviously, good things don't last forever. But in a competitive business environment, you have to be willing to take chances. You can't always live in fear. That said, when things start to look questionable, you also have to be smart enough to know when to get out.[8]

The doom and gloom were justified and the bubble popped two years later but not before Trump founded his own mortgage business in 2006 which had to be shut down the next year.[9] So, it at least looks like he didn't see it coming.

5. On Competition In Education

The State of Our Schools
Posted: 9/8/2005 3:04:00 PM

8. *https://web.archive.org/web/20060507012209/http://donaldtrump.trumpuniversity.com/default.asp?item=98726*
9. http://www.slate.com/blogs/moneybox/2016/02/29/
the_lesson_of_donald_trump_s_failed_sketchy_mortgage_business.html

by **Donald J. Trump**
Chairman, Trump University

Now that Labor Day has come and gone, it's officially back-to-school season. Just in time for a new year of classes, the educational testing and research organization ACT released a report that says only about half of the most recent crop of high school graduates have the reading skills they need to succeed in college. Even fewer are prepared to face college-level science and math classes. That's sobering news.

In a related story, a consortium of some of the world's leading businesses launched a national campaign hoping to better prepare students in science and math. They hope to convince policymakers and the public that America's place in the global economy is at stake.

Meanwhile, the education system is also under relentless attack from politicians as well as teachers, administrators, parents, and students themselves. Everyone has ideas of what's wrong and how to fix it. Some argue that the President's No Child Left Behind Act is so under-funded that states can't implement its mandates. Even if the tools are there to fix our education system, the money isn't.

Yes, funding is critical. But money isn't the only answer and, by far, not the only concern. We can't assume that the only way to fix a problem is by throwing money at it. If we don't have the money, then the problems aren't repairable.

I've spoken in the past about how important it is to give parents a choice as to where they send their kids to school. That way, it challenges all schools–public and private–to ask more of themselves, of their students, and of their teachers. That's one way all schools will improve. When there's choice, there's competition. And competition makes for success all around.

One more thing: get involved. Don't gripe about your child's school if you never walk in the door. Get on the PTA, show up at the teacher conferences, volunteer to be on panels and committees and boards. Invest time in education. Make a commitment. It is the future, you know.[10]

He's been consistent on this issue. If anything, he's even more pro-competition and charter school now[11] than in 2005.

6. On Rebuilding New Orleans After Katrina

In the Wake of Katrina
Posted: 9/20/2005 9:49:00 AM

---

10. *https://web.archive.org/web/20060507022340/*
http://donaldtrump.trumpuniversity.com/default.asp?item=99512
11. http://www.ontheissues.org/2016/Donald_Trump_Education.htm

by **Donald J. Trump**
Chairman, Trump University

There is absolutely no question that we should rebuild New Orleans in the wake of Katrina–even bigger and better than it was before. Although it's difficult to imagine that the once vibrant city will be thriving again, we know cities are resilient. They survive the worst horrors, rebounding from earthquakes, floods and fires as well as wars and worse. Look at how New York City has returned after 9/11.

Right now people are concentrating on the emergency phase. Yet, soon the emphasis will have to be on recovery and rebuilding. The circumstances here are extraordinary. The usual rules hardly apply.

In order for the city to return to its original successful state, business leaders must return to the area. That seems like the right thing to do, but it's not that straightforward and it won't be simple. It would be so much easier to relocate somewhere else rather than wait for a city to be rebuilt from the ground up.

Many businesses with deep ties to the area will make that commitment, but it will be a tough one. It may take years, maybe decades, before the city and its businesses get back to where they were. So those businesses have to realize what lies ahead for them: a painstaking process that won't follow the standard paths of real estate. Who knows how property values will fluctuate or how the values of various locations will change.

Like the people of New Orleans, in the business world, the strong will survive. Many will relocate. Many won't take the chance on rebuilding. That's a shame. About four days before the hurricane we were thinking about building something there with a New Orleans developer as a partner. I look forward to being part of the rebuilding process.[12]

It's hard to tell whether Trump was only for rebuilding New Orleans because he wanted to make money off it or because he felt it was the right thing to do. His most recent statements and actions suggest it was more the former. Trump declined to spend anything on charity to help the city at the time but he's not big on charity in general.[13]

7. Oil Profiteering

Record Oil Prices
Posted: 11/23/2005 11:35:00 AM

---

12. *https://web.archive.org/web/20060507022226/*
http://donaldtrump.trumpuniversity.com/default.asp?item=101792
13. http://newsexaminer.net/politics/donald-trump-the-least-charitable-billionaire/

by **Donald J. Trump**
Chairman, Trump University

Not that long ago, gas prices were at an all-time high, and we were going ballistic. When we were paying as much as $3 a gallon, I couldn't help but direct my anger at oil-producing countries. I was convinced that they were to blame for the soaring costs, and I was angry at our government for not taking more aggressive measures to slow price increases.

Imagine my surprise when the stories came out about how much money the oil companies have been making. While drivers have been paying record prices at the pumps every time they fill their tanks, the oil companies apparently have been making historic profits. It's actually quite unbelievable.

Exxon's profits were up 75 percent to 9.9 billion in the third quarter alone. Shell reported a net income of $9 billion. British Petroleum reported $6.5 billion of profit in the third quarter, and ConocoPhillips reported $3.8 billion. Those are astounding numbers.

I know that the purpose of business is to make money, and I never want to begrudge an organization its profits. But all this time we assumed the oil companies were struggling like the average consumer. This was one time where they could've buckled down just a little bit. They could've taken a little less of a share of the profits so that they wouldn't have passed on such a big burden to the consumers.

Yet here we are, eating the costs of higher oil prices. Something has to be done in Washington.[14]

He's evolved *a lot* on this issue, going so far as to say that we should just "take the oil"[15] presumably from Iraq although it's totally unclear what this actually means. This is basically what every anti-war person in the U.S. feared the Bush administration would do in Iraq but which it didn't do.

8. Outsourcing Of Jobs From The U.S.

Outsourcing Creates Jobs in the Long Run
Posted: 8/29/2005 5:30:00 PM
by **Donald J. Trump**
Chairman, Trump University

We hear terrible things about outsourcing jobs–how sending work outside of our companies is contributing to the demise of American businesses. But in this instance I have

---

14. *https://web.archive.org/web/20060507021038/*
http://donaldtrump.trumpuniversity.com/default.asp?item=114195
15. http://stepfeed.com/more-categories/big-news/donald-trump-ill-invade-syria-destroy-isis-take-oil-u-s/#.Vv7ABRNJkvk

to take the unpopular stance that it is not always a terrible thing.

I understand that outsourcing means that employees lose jobs. Because work is often outsourced to other countries, it means Americans lose jobs. In other cases, nonunion employees get the work. Losing jobs is never a good thing, but we have to look at the bigger picture.

Last year, Nobel Prize-winning economist Dr. Lawrence R. Klein, the founder of Wharton Econometric Forecasting Associates, co-authored a study that showed how global outsourcing actually creates more jobs and increases wages, at least for IT workers. The study found that outsourcing helped companies be more competitive and more productive. That means they make more money, which means they funnel more into the economy, thereby, creating more jobs.

I know that doesn't make it any easier for people whose jobs have been outsourced overseas, but if a company's only means of survival is by farming jobs outside its walls, then sometimes it's a necessary step. The other option might be to close its doors for good.[16]

This has been a lynchpin of Trump's presidential campaign and while his stance on it is 2005 appears to be that it's "some-

16. *https://web.archive.org/web/20060507011645/*
http://donaldtrump.trumpuniversity.com/default.asp?item=98255

times good" his current stance is that it's horrible. Consider this quote[17], also from "Crippled America."

There are people who wish I wouldn't refer to China as our enemy. But that's exactly what they are. They have destroyed entire industries by utilizing low-wage workers, cost us tens of thousands of jobs, spied on our businesses, stolen our technology, and have manipulated and devalued their currency, which makes importing our goods more expensive—and sometimes, impossible.

17. http://stepfeed.com/more-categories/big-news/donald-trump-ill-invade-syria-destroy-isis-take-oil-u-s/#.Vv7ABRNJkvk

8

We Polled Thousands Of Millennials About Their Opinion Of Donald Trump And The Results Are Completely Shocking

Daniel Hayes

In cooperation with the survey professionals from Whatsgoodly, we asked thousands of Millennials about what they thought of Donald Trump. Below are the very interesting results.

1. His Shock Of Hair IS Shocking.

People were more shocked by his hair although "his bullying

comments" came in second place. Male respondents were more shocked by "his bullying comments" than female respondents.

2. Millennials Are Pretty Lukewarm On Both Hillary And Trump.

The "Hillary" and "I'm out" options tied for second place overall. Female responders were much more likely to be dissatisfied with both candidates of these candidates and were also more likely to be for Trump over Hillary.

3. This Was A Trick Question. Trump Has Never Said This.[1]

Respondents answered almost equally to each of the four options provided. The options were:

- They're all criminals
- That he loves Hispanic people and they love him
- He loves their cocaine
- That we shouldn't allow any immigrants into the US

The second option is actually the correct one. Trump has made this claim over and over but he's never suggested not allowing immigrants into the US as a permanent policy.

4. Hillary Clinton Has More Support From Wall Street Than Any Other Candidate.[2]

Male and female respondents were evenly divided here as well

1. https://www.donaldjtrump.com/positions/immigration-reform
2. http://www.opensecrets.org/pres16/indus.php?cycle=2016&id=N00000019&type=f

with "Wall Street loves him" coming in second only three percentage points above "Wall Street hates him."

5. Millennials Believe Trump's Primary Concern Is The Poor.

The responses here were fascinating. 43% of female respondents believe Trump's primary concern is the poor and only 1.7% of female respondents felt immigration was the number one concern. In contrast, 47% of male respondents felt immigration was what he cared about most with only 32% believing Trump cared the most about the poor.

I wrote this survey and never would have guessed this would be the majority response.

6. Millennials Appear To Be Unsure Whether They're Alike Or Think They're Obviously Different.

Very few believe that Trump and Sanders are alike. However, even fewer believe that they are polar opposites. The second most popular answer was "kind of alike" at 22%.

7. Say My (Middle) Name!

89% got this question right. 11% thought that his middle name might be Castillo, Alvarez, or Gonzalez. It is John.

9

OSU Students Respond PERFECTLY To This Pro-Trump Message Chalked On A Campus Sidewalk

Jacob Geers

This morning Ohio State students woke up to an unfortunate message chalked on one of the main sidewalk paths through our campus green space (The Oval).

Students were pretty surprised to see this messaged—that was chalked in the dark of night—scrawled out on campus the day before OSU's biggest visitation day of the year.

But how people responded was absolutely incredible.

Students from all corners of campus and walks of life came

Twitter

together to chalk over the message with colorful pictures and phrases of love, acceptance, tolerance, and diversity.

And some of the messages are really quite touching.

My fellow OSU students kept chalking message of love until the ugly "Build The Wall" message is barely even visible.

I talked to Hanna Detwiler, a friend who participated in the event *and* took many of these awesome pictures:

> *I saw a picture of the Trump drawing so I went to go check it out and a group of students were chalking positive messages all over it. Of course I had to join in! Free speech goes both ways.*
>
> *You can say whatever you want, but people can reciprocate*

Facebook / Hanna Detwiler

that as well. You can say something racist, but that doesn't mean people aren't allowed to retaliate in an equally peaceful way. You want to spread the hate, we'll spread the love, obviously you can see what's more popular.

And maybe this is how things get better. Not by pretending hate doesn't exist, or yelling about hate at the top of our lungs—but by simply covering it up with love.

Love Trumps Hate. At OSU, and everywhere.

Facebook / Hanna Detwiler

Facebook / Hanna Detwiler

10

Everything You Ever Wanted To Know About Political Conventions And The 2016 Election

Jacob Geers

Alrighty folks, even if you aren't super political you've probably heard all the banter surrounding the United States' very very strange 2016 election. I am here to distil all the nonsense and prognostications and give (I hope) a very simple guide to what the heck is going on:

What is a political party convention?

A convention is like a huge meeting of the party to decide on important business. It's at the convention where parties vote on their official platform, elect various officers, and of course, select their Presidential candidate for the next November.

So wait, the convention picks the Presidential candidate for each party?

Yes.

So like, what are all these primaries and caucuses for then?

Primaries and caucuses elect delegates—the people who attend the convention. So when you vote for a Presidential candidate, you are voting for a delegate who is promising to vote for that said candidate at the Convention.

Wait, I'm still confused!

Okay, no problem, because it is super confusing.

Back in the good ole days, the party conventions did everything and "the people" really had very little say in who attended the conventions and what exactly they did. The convention was just made up of party leaders and handpicked people. There were no primaries or caucuses in the same way we see today.

Over time, however, people weren't crazy about this system (for understandable reasons) and slowly, each party started giving some of the power to select delegates to "the people" via primaries and caucuses. The convention itself is really a relic of that old process.

So are political conventions "democratic?"

For the most part, yes. The conventions are filled with delegates that YOU elected to represent your interests. You might not know the specific delegates and their issues, but they represent your candidate (and in theory) their positions on policy. It isn't a direct democracy, but hey, it works...usually.

What about "superdelegates?"

So, in the **Democratic Party** only, roughly 20% of the delegates (the people who ultimately chose the nominee) are "superdelegates." These individuals have the right to vote for ANY candidate, regardless of how their state votes.

The argument for their role in the process is that the party leadership should have a say in who is selected, particularly in evaluating how "good of a Democrat" a Presidential candidate might be.

Others say that superdelegates are undemocratic because they can do whatever they want. In reality, they are just a relic of a procedure that was once mostly undemocratic and is now mostly democratic.

Okay, so what is this talk about a "brokered" or "contested" convention?

So to be a political party's nominee you must with a majority of the delegates. That is to say, you must have 50% + 1 delegates vote for you at the Republican convention to be the Republican candidate for President, and 50% + 1 delegates vote for you at the Democratic party convention to be the Democratic nominee for President.

If you have that 50% + 1 (a majority) there is NOTHING the party can do to stop you from being the nominee. There is no contested convention, nothing like that. If you win a majority, you are golden.

BUT, if you don't have a majority, that's when things get tricky. **Having the *most* votes is not enough.** You need a majority. If you don't have a majority, the party keeps voting until someone finds a majority.

How does that happen?

So, there are different "rounds" of voting.

In the first round, all elected delegates (pledged delegates) MUST vote for the candidate they were elected to represent. In the Democratic Party, of course, the "superdelegates" are still, and always, free to vote for whoever they want.

But then things get interesting. On the second ballot, some delegates are released from their "pledge" to vote for the candidate they were elected to represent. Legally, they can vote for whoever they want.

On the third ballot, almost all delegates are totally free to vote for whoever they want, without ANY regard for how their state voted.

A "contested" or "brokered" convention is just a convention where we go in not knowing the winner.

Is that democratic? Is that fair?

I mean, I think it depends on how you look at it. On first glance, it does seem a little unfair that the candidate with the most votes doesn't win outright, but there's another very important way to look at it.

Let's say we go into a political convention with these candidates who have the following number of votes. Totally making these numbers up:

FIRST BALLOT

Kendra Syrdal: *40*

Chrissy Stockton: *30*

Daniel Hayes: *20*

Mélanie Berliet: *10*

TOTAL: *100 delegates (51 required for majority)*

Okay, so Kendra obviously has the most delegates going into the convention. So if the winner was just the person who had the "most" she would be the nominee. On first glance, that might seem like the fairest outcome. But she doesn't have a majority.

But maybe the delegates from Melanie knows that she doesn't really have a chance, and decide to jump ship to support Chrissy because Chrissy is their second choice:

SECOND BALLOT

Kendra Syrdal: *40*

Chrissy Stockton: *40*

Daniel Hayes: *20*

Mélanie Berliet: *0*

TOTAL: *100 delegates (51 required for majority)*

Okay, so still nobody has a majority. And let's say that Daniel Hayes' supporters also realize he probably isn't going to be the nominee, and let's say the split 40% for Kendra, and 60% for Chrissy:

THIRD BALLOT

Chrissy Stockton: *52*

Kendra Syrdal: *48*

Daniel Hayes: *0*

Mélanie Berliet: *0*

TOTAL: *100 delegates (51 required for majority)*

And so, as it turns out, despite being in second when the convention started, Chrissy has over 50% of the delegates and is the nominee. In some ways, this system is fairer because it allows the delegates of the "losing" candidates to take their second choice into consideration. It expands representation and prevents "dead votes" for third and fourth place candidates from being totally disregarded. When we only ask who has the **MOST votes** the only two candidates whose votes matter are the top two. Anyone who voted for anyone else gets cut out of the equation.

Hmm, I still think that's a little undemocratic

That's fair. Unlike in math and science, there are no "right" answers here. I'm just trying to explain the other side.

So does this mean that Donald Trump or Hillary Clinton could still lose their parties' nominations?

Yes to Donald, and maybe to Hillary.

Hillary is fairly safe because of the "superdelegates" who are *likely* to pile onto her at the convention because she is also leading in the elected, or pledged delegates.

The Donald, however, is also leading in elected delegates but because of how many different Republican candidates ran and collected delegates, he is VERY unlikely (but not impossible) to get a majority. What happens at a Republican Convention where he doesn't have a majority of the delegates is anybody's guess.

11

We Dug Through 21 Ancient Donald Trump Tweets, And It Turns Out He's Always Been Insane

Kim Quindlen

1. Remember when Trump got in on the Kristen Stewart/Robert Pattinson drama? Now you do.

So many tweets & stories on Stewart/Pattinson Look, it doesn't matter– the relationship will never be the same. It is permanently broken.

— Donald J. Trump (@realDonaldTrump) October 19, 2012

2. And he just keeps going.

Everyone knows I am right that Robert Pattinson should dump Kristen Stewart. In a couple of years, he will thank me. Be smart, Robert.

— Donald J. Trump (@realDonaldTrump) October 22, 2012

3. Literally, there are like 6 of these lol.

After Friday's Twilight release, I hope Robert Pattinson will not be seen in public with Kristen–she will cheat on him again!

— Donald J. Trump (@realDonaldTrump) November 13, 2012

4. Hey Donald, what's your wig made out of? YOUR MOM'S CHEST HAIR.

As everybody knows, but the haters & losers refuse to acknowledge, I do not wear a "wig." My hair may not be perfect but it's mine.

— Donald J. Trump (@realDonaldTrump) April 24, 2013

----

5. What.... even is this tweet?

It's Friday. How many bald eagles did wind turbines kill today? They are an environmental & aesthetic disaster.

— Donald J. Trump (@realDonaldTrump) August 24, 2012

----

6. Musings of the Donald.

I have never seen a thin person drinking Diet Coke.

— Donald J. Trump (@realDonaldTrump) October 14, 2012

7. Go home, Trump. You're drunk.

The concept of global warming was created by and for the Chinese in order to make U.S. manufacturing non-competitive.

— Donald J. Trump (@realDonaldTrump) November 6, 2012

8. Anything 'environmentally friendly' is DANGEROUS.

Remember, new "environment friendly" lightbulbs can cause cancer. Be careful– the idiots who came up with this stuff don't care.

— Donald J. Trump (@realDonaldTrump) October 17, 2012

9. No.

Why is Obama playing basketball today? That is why our country is in trouble!

— Donald J. Trump (@realDonaldTrump) November 6, 2012

———————

10. Goodbye.

While @BetteMidler is an extremely unattractive woman, I refuse to say that because I always insist on being politically correct.

— Donald J. Trump (@realDonaldTrump) October 28, 2012

———————

11. Sure, people who try to save others are nice, but they must be punished.

The U.S. cannot allow EBOLA infected people back. Peo-

ple that go to far away places to help out are great-but must suffer the consequences!

— Donald J. Trump (@realDonaldTrump) August 2, 2014

---

12. Donald Trump, future Hallmark greeting card writer.

I would like to wish everyone, including all haters and losers (of which, sadly, there are many) a truly happy and enjoyable Memorial Day!

— Donald J. Trump (@realDonaldTrump) May 24, 2015

---

13. He even ruins his own attempts to be respectful.

"@realDonaldTrump: I would like to extend my best wishes to all, even the haters and losers, on this special date, September 11th."

— Donald J. Trump (@realDonaldTrump) September 12, 2013

---

14. Ugh.

An 'extremely credible source' has called my office and told me that @BarackObama's birth certificate is a fraud.

— Donald J. Trump (@realDonaldTrump) August 6, 2012

––––––––––

15. This guy sure knows how to negotiate.

If Obama resigns from office NOW, thereby doing a great service to the country—I will give him free lifetime golf at any one of my courses!

— Donald J. Trump (@realDonaldTrump) September 10, 2014

––––––––––

16. Nope.

My twitter has become so powerful that I can actually make my enemies tell the truth.

— Donald J. Trump (@realDonaldTrump) October 17, 2012

---

17. This is how science works, kids.

Healthy young child goes to doctor, gets pumped with massive shot of many vaccines, doesn't feel good and changes – AUTISM. Many such cases!

— Donald J. Trump (@realDonaldTrump) March 28, 2014

---

18. NO.

26,000 unreported sexual assults in the military-only 238 convictions. What did these geniuses expect when they put men & women together?

— Donald J. Trump (@realDonaldTrump) May 7, 2013

---

19. Stop.

Wind turbines are not only killing millions of birds, they are killing the finances & environment of many countries & communities.

— Donald J. Trump (@realDonaldTrump) October 17, 2012

---

20. One more on Robert and Kristen, for good luck.

Everyone is asking me to speak more on Robert & Kristen. I don't have time except to say "Robert, drop her, she cheated on you & will again!"

— Donald J. Trump (@realDonaldTrump) October 23, 2012

---

21. 'Tiny Children Are Not Horses' NEW BAND NAME I CALL IT.

No more massive injections. Tiny children are not horses—one vaccine at a time, over time.

— Donald J. Trump (@realDonaldTrump) September 3, 2014

12

This Is How The 2016 Election Would End If Millennials Were The Only Voters

Daniel Hayes

If young people were the only ones voting in the Democratic Primary, then Bernie Sanders would win by a landslide. But why? Let's take a look at voter impressions by region and on the issues below.

HOW IT GENERALLY BREAKS DOWN BY SCHOOL AND REGION

The Southern schools polled generally were more likely to be pro-Clinton while the West Coast and the Midwest leaned towards Sanders. Of the Northeastern school polled, it leaned slightly towards Clinton. Here's a sample of colleges from across the country.

The South

Southern Methodist University

Clinton: 61.3%
Sanders: 38.7%

Vanderbilt University

Clinton: 61.9%
Sanders: 38.1%

The Midwest

University of Wisconsin-Madison

Clinton: 34.9%
Sanders 65.1%

University of Illinois

Clinton: 25%
Sanders: 75%

The West Coast

University of California-Berkeley

Clinton: 48.4%
Sanders: 51.6%

The Northeast

University of Pennsylvania

Clinton: 50.8%
Sanders: 49.2%

HERE'S HOW YOUNG VOTERS FELT ABOUT THE ELECTION AND CANDIDATES IN MORE DETAIL

There are some surprises here. Nearly half of Sanders voters refuse to vote for Clinton in the general which isn't terribly surprising given the Bernie or Bust movement. What's very surprising is that Clinton voters feel the *exact same way* despite not having a hashtag for it. Data all via Whatsgoodly[1] polling.

1. NEARLY HALF OF SANDERS VOTERS WON'T VOTE CLINTON

"If Sanders doesn't win the nomination what will you do?"

(3,813 Overall Votes)

- **53%** – Vote for Clinton **(2,040 votes)**
- **27%** – Vote for Trump (because F it) **(1,021 votes)**
- **11%** – Vote for a third party ("go ahead, throw your vote away") **(421 votes)**
- **9%** – Not vote and also leave the country forever **(331 votes)**

---

1. https://bnc.lt/whatsgoodlyinsights

Male – 2,150 Total Votes

- Vote for Clinton (968 votes)
- Vote for Trump (because F it) (744 votes)
- Vote for a third party ("go ahead, throw your vote away") (265 votes)
- Not vote and also leave the country forever (173 votes)

Female – 1,663 Total Votes

- Vote for Clinton (1,072 votes)
- Vote for Trump (because F it) (277 votes)
- Vote for a third party ("go ahead, throw your vote away") (156 votes)
- Not vote and also leave the country forever (158 votes)

2. NEARLY HALF OF CLINTON VOTERS WON'T VOTE FOR SANDERS

If Clinton doesn't win the nomination what will you do?

(4,450 Overall Votes)

- **54%** – Vote for Sanders **(2,420 votes)**
- **27%** – Vote for Trump (because F it) **(1,152 votes)**
- **10%** – Vote for a third party ("go ahead, throw your vote away") **(475 votes)**
- **9%** – Not vote and also leave the country forever **(403 votes)**

Male – 2,575 Total Votes

- Vote for Sanders (1,264 votes)
- Vote for Trump (because F it) (835 votes)
- Vote for a third party ("go ahead, throw your vote away") (288 votes)
- Not vote and also leave the country forever (188 votes)

Female – 1,875 Total Votes

- Vote for Sanders (1,156 votes)
- Vote for Trump (because F it) (317 votes)
- Vote for a third party ("go ahead, throw your vote away") (187 votes)
- Not vote and also leave the country forever (215 votes)

3. CLINTON VOTERS LESS CONCERNED ABOUT HER BEING A WOMAN AND MORE FOCUSED ON EXPERIENCE

"If you're pro-Clinton what appeals to you most about her?"

(2,526 Overall Votes)

- **13%** – Her career focus on women's issues (**332 votes**)
- **37%** – Her experience as a Senator and Secretary of State (**932 votes**)
- **22%** – She's the best candidate to defeat the GOP (**564 votes**)
- **28%** – The idea that she's the candidate that can actually get stuff done (**698 votes**)

Male – 1,393 Total Votes

- Her career focus on women's issues (143 votes)
- Her experience as a Senator and Secretary of State (525 votes)
- She's the best candidate to defeat the GOP (330 votes)
- The idea that she's the candidate that can actually get stuff done (395 votes)

Female – 1,133 Total Votes

- Her career focus on women's issues (189 votes)
- Her experience as a Senator and Secretary of State (407 votes)
- She's the best candidate to defeat the GOP (234 votes)
- The idea that she's the candidate that can actually get stuff done (303 votes)

4. DEMOCRATS AREN'T PLEASED WITH THE CANDIDATES THIS YEAR

"Democratic voters, do you like this year's Presidential choices overall?"

(6,301 Overall Votes)

- **7%** – Yes, they're great **(423 votes)**
- **21%** – They're okay **(1,331 votes)**
- **27%** – They're pretty weak **(1,713 votes)**
- **45%** – Worst in my lifetime **(2,834 votes)**

Male – 4,474 Total Votes

- Yes, they're great (309 votes)

- They're okay (878 votes)
- They're pretty weak (1,228 votes)
- Worst in my lifetime (2,059 votes)

Female – 1,827 Total Votes

- Yes, they're great (114 votes)
- They're okay (453 votes)
- They're pretty weak (485 votes)
- Worst in my lifetime (775 votes)

5. SANDERS VOTERS LOVE HIS INDEPENDENCE MORE THAN ANYTHING ELSE

"If you're pro-Sanders what appeals to you most about him?"

(2,980 Overall Votes)

- **16%** – Universal public college (**481 votes**)
- **11%** – Single-payer healthcare (**315 votes**)
- **15%** – His plan to bring jobs back to the states correctly (**454 votes**)
- **58%** – The impression (fact?) that he can't be bought (**698 votes**)

Male – 1,801 Total Votes

- Universal public college (259 votes)
- Single-payer healthcare (203 votes)
- His plan to bring jobs back to the states correctly (234 votes)

- The impression (fact?) that he can't be bought (1,105 votes)

Female – 1,179 Total Votes

- Universal public college (222 votes)
- Single-payer healthcare (112 votes)
- His plan to bring jobs back to the states correctly (220 votes)
- The impression (fact?) that he can't be bought (625 votes)

6. EVEN CLINTON VOTERS TRUST SANDERS THE MOST

"Democratic voters, who do you trust to try and do what they say?"

(5,314 Overall Votes)

- **40%** – Sanders **(2,107 votes)**
- **17%** – Clinton **(941 votes)**
- **13%** – Trump **(665 votes)**
- **30%** – I'm not a Democrat **(1,601 votes)**

Male – 3,123 Total Votes

- Sanders (1,244 votes)
- Clinton (411 votes)
- Trump (528 votes)
- I'm not a Democrat (940 votes)

Female – 2,191 Total Votes

- Sanders (863 votes)
- Clinton (530 votes)
- Trump (137 votes)
- I'm not a Democrat (661 votes)

19 Questions To Ask When You're Wondering If He's A Trump Bro

Katie Mather

1. Is his favorite country song "Wagon Wheel"?

2. Does he scream the lyrics at the top of his lungs when he's drunk, with one arm thrown around the neck of the closest stranger to him?

3. Has he told you he's voting for Trump because "he's not Hillary"?

4. Has he mentioned that he "hates politicians"?

5. Did he tell you more than once that he thinks taxes are dumb—even though his signing bonus for that consulting job he got at his dad's firm immediately after graduating from Bucknell is greater than the annual income of the average working class family?

6. Does he look like the type who would drink a margarita out of a can on Metro North?

7. Is his name something like Brad? Or Brock? Is he, like, the third Brad or Brock in his family?

8. Is he doing an extraordinary amount of mansplaining to you?

9. How long has he spent describing his Ideal Woman to you?

10. Does he say things like "misogyny isn't an issue today"?[1]

11. Did he just misuse the words "socialist" or "fascist"?

12. Are you watching him argue with someone? Did he just ungracefully lose said argument and call his opponent "so fucking gay"?

13. How many times has he mentioned "plowing chicks"? How little do you believe that he's been doing anything of the sort?

14. Does he have a strong opinion on when it's appropriate for himself to wear blue jeans? Is that time when he's either on a farm or when he's feeling too casual for his perpetually pleated khakis?

15. Look at his Facebook. How many of his profile pictures are of him playing lacrosse?

16. Look at his Instagram. How many of his pictures are of him, shirtless with American flag swim trunks, barbecuing meat?

1. http://www.cbsnews.com/news/meet-the-trump-bros/

17. Has he reminded you that Trump "is the only candidate who won't destroy America"?

18. When asked by you to further clarify that statement with legitimate, factual evidence in your feeble attempt to have a real conversation with this person, did he just start shouting "'MERICA"?

19. Is he riveted and relieved by Trump's anti-PC rhetoric? Does he think being politically correct is the same as being censored? Did he bring up the wrong amendment ("it's the third one or whatever") as proof that being PC is anti-American?

PART 3

Donald Trump is now the Republican nominee. Last ditch efforts to unseat him at the Republican Convention have failed, and he has tapped Indiana Governor Mike Pence to be his running mate.

For the next few months, a fierce debate will begin to tear at the nation's seams. Polls will have Trump consistently down through August, but he will begin to regain ground in early September with stories of the Clinton Foundation and Hillary Clinton's private email server consuming the media discourse.

14

YIKES: Mike Pence Says 'Mulan' Is Proof That Women Shouldn't Be Allowed In The Military

Jacob Geers

Mike Pence, the not-so-honorable running mate of Donald Trump was seen by many as the "safe choice" for Vice President. Reports have surfaced that "The Donald" really didn't want Pence onboard, and preferred someone more outrightly nuts, like Chris Christie or Newt Gingrich.

However, Trump might be relieved by news coming in of some of the *ridiculous* things that Mike Pence has said (and believes). An example? **Mike Pence once used the Disney movie Mulan as "proof" that women should not be in the military.** He begins with this absurd summary:

"Just spent a memorable Fathers Day, like so many other all American Hoosier dads, with my kids at the new Disney film entitled, "Mulan". For those who have not yet been victimized by the McDonald's induced hysteria over this film, Mulan is a fictional account of a delicate girl of the same name who surreptitiously takes her fathers place in the Chinese army in one of their ancient wars against the Huns."

Delicate? I think anybody who watched the movie could reasonably conclude that Mulan would probably kick Mike Pence's ass.

Anyway, he moves on with some social commentary (that nobody asked for):

"Despite her delicate features and voice, Disney expects us to believe that Mulan's ingenuity and courage were enough to carry her to military success on an equal basis with her cloddish cohorts. Obviously, this is Walt Disney's attempt to add childhood expectation to the cultural debate over the role of women in the military. I suspect that some mischievous liberal at Disney assumes that Mulan's story will cause a quiet change in the next generation's attitude about women in combat."

Yikes, yikes, yikes. **But it gets worse.**

Pence goes on in the letter to essentially claim that women should not be in the military because men sexually assault them.

"The only problem with this liberal hope is the reality which intrudes on the Disney ideal from the mornings headlines. From the original "Tailhook" scandal involving scores of high ranking navy fighter pilots who molested subordinate women to the latest travesty at Aberdeen Proving Grounds, the hard truth of our experiment with gender integration is that is has been an almost complete disaster for the military and for many of the individual women involved."

Basically, shaming the victims here and saying that it is the "system's" fault if they get sexually assaulted. According to this, women shouldn't be in the military because men attack them—yeah, that makes a TON of sense (it doesn't).

Anyway, you can read the full text of Pence's op-ed piece below:

Just spent a memorable Fathers Day, like so many other all American Hoosier dads, with my kids at the new Disney film entitled, "Mulan". For those who have not yet been victimized by the McDonald's induced hysteria over this film, Mulan is a fictional account of a delicate girl of the same name who surreptitiously takes her fathers place in the Chinese army in one of their ancient wars against the Huns. Despite her delicate features and voice, Disney expects us to believe that Mulan's ingenuity and courage were enough to carry her to military success on an equal basis with her cloddish cohorts. Obviously, this is Walt Disney's attempt to add childhood expectation to the cultural debate over the role of women in the military. I suspect that some mischievous liberal at Disney assumes that Mulan's story will cause a quiet change in the next generation's attitude about women in combat and they just might be right. (Just think about how often we think of Bambi every time the subject of deer hunting comes into the mainstream media debate.)

The only problem with this liberal hope is the reality which intrudes on the Disney ideal from the mornings headlines. From the original "Tailhook" scandal involving scores of high ranking navy fighter pilots who molested subordinate women to the latest travesty at Aberdeen Proving Grounds, the hard truth of our experiment with gender integration is that is has been an almost complete disaster for the military and for many of the individual women involved. When Indiana Congressman Steve Buyer was appointed to investigate the Aberdeen mess, he shocked the public with the revelation that young, nubile, 18 year old men and women were actually being HOUSED together during basic training. Whatever bone head came up with this idea should be run out of this man's Army before sundown. Housing, in close quarters, young men and women (in some cases married to non-military personnel) at the height of their physical and sexual potential is the height of stupidity. It is instructive that even in the Disney film, young Ms. Mulan falls in love with her superior officer!

Me thinks the politically correct Disney types completely missed the irony of this part of the story. They likely added it because it added realism with which the viewer could identify with the characters. You see, now stay with me on this, many young men find many young women to be attractive sexually. Many young women find many young men to be attractive sexually. Put them together, in close quarters, for long periods of time, and things will get interesting. Just like they eventually did for young Mulan. Moral of story: women in military, bad idea.

15

It Looks Like Melania Trump Plagiarized Michelle Obama In Her RNC Address Tonight

Jacob Geers

This evening Melania Trump spoke before the 2016 Republican National Convention to shower praise on her husband Donald Trump.

However, her words may not all be her own.

As noticed by Journalist Jarrett Hill, several paragraphs of her text bears an almost identical resemblance to a large portion of Michelle Obama's 2008 speech.

Here is Michelle's speech from 2008:

And you know, what struck me when I first met Barack was that even though he had this funny name, even though he'd grown up all the way across the continent in Hawaii, his family was so much like mine. He was raised by grandparents who were working-class folks just like my parents, and by a single mather who struggled to pay the bills just like we did. Like my famly, they scrimped and saved so that he could have opportunities they never had themselves. AND BARACK AND I WERE RAISED WITH SO MANY OF THE SAME VALUES: THAT YOU WORK HARD FOR WHAT YOU WANT IN LIFE; THAT YOUR WORDS IS YOUR BOND AND DO WHAT YOU SAY YOU'RE GOING TO DO; THAT YOU TREAT PEOPLE WITH DIGNITY AND RESPECT, EVEN IN YOU DON'T KNOW THEM, AND EVEN IF YOU DON'T AGREE WITH THEM.

AND BARACK AND I SET OUT TO BUILD LIVES GUIDED BY THESE VALUES, ADN PASS THEM ON TO THE NEXT GENERATION. BECAUSE WE WANT OUR CHILDREN—AND ALL CHILDREN IN THIS NATION—TO KNOW THAT THE ONLY LIMIT TO THE HEIGHT OF YOUR ACHIEVEMENTS IS THE REACH OF YOUR DREAMS AND YOUR WILLINGNESS TO WORK FOR THEM.[1]

Compare the highlighted portions with Melania's address

---

1. https://twitter.com/JarrettHill/status/755242423991709697?lang=en

tonight: https://www.youtube.com/
watch?v=53Ei2dSDsFY&feature=youtu.be&t=2m4s

Melania has told NBC News that she "wrote the speech" and
had "as little help as possible":

Does this mean she takes responsibility for the error?

*VIDEO: Melania Trump told NBC's Matt Lauer before
the speech: "I wrote it…with a little help as possible."
https://t.co/MZraa04Goj*

— Bradd Jaffy (@BraddJaffy) July 19, 2016

Wow! Certainly not something you would expect from such a
family of savvy business minds…

16

Ted Cruz's Tender Heart Was Broken After Being Booed At RNC Convention

Jacob Geers

Ted Cruz—a vicious opponent of Donald Trump in the GOP primary—exchanged many vitriolic attacks with the presumptive nominee during the campaign. Many people expected him to finally throw his support behind Trump, but he didn't.

Instead, Cruz told people to "vote their conscience," which is exactly when the booing began—starting with the New York delegation.

The booing continued as they were subjected to hearing more audible words from Ted Cruz that were not in full devotion of Overlord Trump.

At the end of Ted Cruz's speech, Donald Trump entered the

arena, fully diverting attention from the despondent Cruz to the nominee himself. Cruz then began his lonely trudge off the stage, brokenhearted, to the sound of people booing and his few diehard supporters urging him to carry on.

17

George Harrison's Facebook Account Had This HILARIOUS Response To Donald Trump Using Their Song

Jacob Geers

Tonight at the Republican National Convention Donald Trump's party used the song, "Here Comes the Sun."

George Harrison's successors—who run his Facebook account—says that they did not approve of the use.

BUT they might have approved of another song being used…

Politicians often get in trouble for using songs without authorization, but musicians very rarely take action. Just this year, however, Mike Huckabee had to pay $25,000 for his unauthorized use of "Eye of the Tiger."

George Harrison
52 mins ·

The unauthorized use of #HereComestheSun at the #RNCinCLE is offensive & against the wishes of the George Harrison estate.

If it had been "Beware of Darkness" then we MAY have approved it!

#TrumpYourself

Facebook

18

Donald Trump Says Barack Obama Is The Founder Of ISIS (He's Not)

Jacob Geers

Republican Presidential nominee Donald J. Trump suggested yesterday that Barack Obama is literally the founder of ISIS—a terror organization that has killed hundreds, if not thousands, of innocent people all around the world.

> *"In fact, in many respects, they honor President Obama. ISIS is honoring Obama. He is the founder of ISIS."*

Now, Trump has made comments like this before. And usually he is straightened out by his legion of advisors and comes out and clarifies what he "actually" meant. However, Trump is standing by the literal meaning of what he said here.

Trump had a radio interview with conservative talk show host Hugh Hewitt, who generously tried to clarify the remarks.

Hewitt explained that his interpretation of the remarks was, "that [Obama] created the vacuum, he lost the peace," and THAT action was what brought up the rise of ISIS.

Trump, however, is having none of it. He waves away Hewitt's interpretation, and insists that Obama is ISIS' actual founder:

"No, I meant he's the founder of ISIS. I do. He was the most valuable player. I give him the most valuable player award. I give her, too, by the way, Hillary Clinton."

For the record, Barack Obama is not the founder of ISIS. That would be Abu Musab al-Zarqawi, who rallied anti-United States forces into a coalition in 2006. This group eventually became the organization we know today as ISIS or ISIL.

19

Hey Dad, Here Are 49 More Reasons Why You Shouldn't Vote For Donald Trump

Ryan Holiday

Hey Dad,

Last time we talked about Donald Trump was right before I published my letter to you about him, "Dear Dad, Please Don't Vote For Donald Trump." I told you that there had been some pushback about publishing it and out of concern you asked me, "You know, are you sure you really want the trouble?" I told you I was ready for it, but of course, I only had a vague idea of what I was getting myself into.

The letter brought on the army of Trump trolls (many of whom are clearly fake, Russian accounts) and I got a number of nasty emails from readers of mine telling me they were leaving and never coming back. Some media drama followed as well—the letter was covered by *Politico* and *Newsmax* and *Forward*. It was weird to see one of my colleagues at the *Observer* describe my writing as 'navel gazing', and hearing that suddenly the entire genre of open letters was being banned from the paper.

At the same time, the response was far greater than I expected. A number of people I never expected to get emails from reached out. I was most touched by the folks who told they were using the letter to have a conversation with their own parents. The letter has been read close to a million times now and gotten hundreds of comments from all over the world (arguably more people saw it this way than if it has just been published as a normal column). Someone is even trying to turn the letter into a short film.

One of the things you told me after you'd read the letter—I'd wanted you to read it before I published it or it wouldn't have been a real letter—was that it had given you a lot to think about. That was all I was hoping for. I just wanted you to hear me and it means a lot to me that you did.

But I also know that you haven't made up your mind yet. That's fair. The race isn't over yet, and some things have happened that are worth considering. Since then, we've seen two political conventions, a massive email hack/leak, and given our insane media system, an endless cycle of news, scandals, and controversies. I've been in three different countries since that letter was published, traveled to the West Coast, the Midwest and the Deep South. I've talked to hundreds of people and despite attempting to ignore the news, watched way too much of it. Almost every interview I do now, even when they are about my books, comes back to Trump in some way. All of this has given me a lot to think about too.

Given that you are still making up your mind, I thought I would put together some more points that I hope you consider. I haven't changed my mind, though I still am hoping to change yours. Regardless of what the poll numbers say, every eligible citizen is faced with a moral choice in November: Should they vote? Should they vote for a third party candidate? Should they vote for a candidate they disagree with simply because they disagree with another candidate more? *Should they vote for Donald Trump?* I'd encourage you to say "no" to that last question—and here are some more reasons why:

1. As you probably heard, Donald Trump claimed that Obama was the founder of ISIS. His exact words: "[Obama] is the founder of ISIS. He is the founder of ISIS, okay? He is the founder. He founded ISIS. And I would say the co-founder would be crooked Hillary Clinton." Obviously, this is not true—but look, sometimes we get carried away when we're talking. Yet when he had the opportunity to backtrack this with Hugh Hewitt, Trump insisted: "No, I meant he's the founder of ISIS." Then he did backtrack later, by saying (like a child in all caps) "THEY DON'T GET SARCASM?". Then in Pennsylvania, he said it was "Not that sarcastic, to be honest with you." This is what our foreign policy is going to come to, a parsing of what is and isn't sarcastic?

2. In recent security briefings, Trump is said to have repeatedly asked why the US can't or doesn't use its nuclear weapons. I urge you to read security analyst John Noonan's series of tweets about what it means to actually use nuclear weapons. In the case that the president demands their use, there is no one who can intervene. You've seen the kind of radical vacillation that Trump seems to undergo on a daily basis, you've seen the emotional, impulsive responses he has to attacks and insults. You also saw his answers in an early debate where he seems to not know what the "nuclear triad" is—something that can be learned easily from, ahem, Wikipedia or a History Channel documentary. Forget the Supreme Court, I'm not sure this is the guy to put in charge of the world's most powerful nuclear arsenal.

3. But surely calmer heads would prevail if Trump made a dangerous decision about the deployment of nuclear arms right? Let me remind you what he said earlier this year in regards to military personnel following his potential orders to use torture techniques (also a potential war crime): "They won't refuse. They're not going to refuse me. If I say do it, they're going to do it."

4. Regardless of what you think of their decision to get involved in politics, Khizr Khan and his wife Ghazala gave one of the most touching speeches of the DNC. Hardly on shaky ground, they questioned the constitutionality of Trump's proposed Muslim ban and spoke of the memory of their fallen son—a man who heroically died in our armed forces. Donald's response? In an interview with George Stephanopoulos he insulted their religion, insinuated that they hadn't written their own speech and questioned whether Ghazala Khan had been forbidden to speak by her husband ("A lot of people have said that," he claimed. Really? Who?) All he could have said was, "I thank them for their sacrifice." Instead, Trump attacked and then later, doubled down on his insults. Then his son lied and claimed that his father had apologized (to date, he *still* has not apologized). Then Trump's New York campaign co-chair remarked that Khizr Khan doesn't deserve the Gold Star title because he dared to question the Trumps. If you have a second, read this *New York Times* piece about the Khan family and their sacrifice. I read it last week and actually cried. How does this family not represent the very best about America? How has it come to the point where the Republican party's nominee for President can attack the patriotism of a family whose son *died* fighting for this country?

5. I think one line in Trump's response stands out best: "While I feel deeply for the loss of his son, Mr. Khan who has never met me, has no right to stand in front of millions of people and claim I have never read the Constitution, (which is false) and say many other inaccurate things." Perhaps Donald Trump has read the Constitution, but I'm not sure he understands it the way that you taught me to.

6. Remember when Hillary said that "a man you can bait with a tweet is not a man we can trust with nuclear weapons." That was a pretty basic political trap. To beat it—to make his opponent look bad—all Trump had to do was *not* say emotional or dumb things on Twitter. And yet, here we are…

7. As the *New York Times* reported, Trump's campaign chairman, Paul Manafort has allegedly received nearly $13 million in cash payments from Ukraine's pro-Russian political party during his time as a political consultant there. Nor has Manafort cleared up whether his has any continued business relationships with foreign powers—and according to the *New York Times*, his aides were still working in the Ukraine *as recently as* *this year.* The guy's stuff is still in his office! But Mike Pence said that's all FINE because Manafort is not running for president."

8. As a person who taught me to own my words and say what I mean, I have to imagine you find Trump's tendency to use the phrase 'many people are saying' as a way to cast aspersions and make insinuations as cowardly and dishonest. I'm no fan of political correctness and I think people should be blunt—but bluntness doesn't mean you get to choose your own facts (or worse, *pretend other people are the ones saying what you are making up*). I don't remember you or Mom ever letting me get away with "Many people say" in my homework or essays I wrote from school. You said it many times: "Cite your sources."

9. Trump still hasn't released his tax returns. Even though his campaign manager taunted Mitt Romney for not fully releasing his. Even though back in 2014, Trump himself said: "If I decide to run for office, I'll produce my tax returns, absolutely, and I would love to do that." Well, where are they?

10. Is he still unwilling to release them because, as many people are saying, he has donated to NAMBLA, an advocacy group for pedophiles? I don't know, but I *do know* that I've seen a lot of chatter about that on the internet. That's what they're saying, so there must be something to it.

11. "Russia, if you're listening, I hope you're able to find the 30,000 emails that are missing," Trump said during a news conference. Can you imagine? A potential head of state calling for a belligerent foreign power to intervene in our affairs, to leak supposedly classified information because it would embarrass his opponent?

12. I'm sure you saw this video of Trump's comments about Clinton and the Supreme Court. We both know that the media has an interest in turning offhand comments into scandals but it's hard not to see what his insinuation was here. He was joking that people with guns could take care of Hillary. He was joking about someone killing his opponent (this is not so far-fetched—early this year Jo Cox was killed in the UK for her campaign against Brexit). The crowd certainly got the dark meaning of his joke—that's why they laughed.

13. The whole thing about Trump actually being in bed with Putin is a little far-fetched, I agree. But isn't it a little bit weird that just this week his daughter posted a travel photo of her and *someone who literally is in bed with Putin.* When she isn't stumping for her dad, Ivanka apparently thinks it's a good idea to go on vacation with Wendi Murdoch, who is allegedly dating Vladimir Putin, and take photos of it. Brilliant!

14. Donald's own spokesperson, Katrina Pierson said that it was Obama who took the U.S. to Afghanistan. Uhh, what? Later, she blamed the preposterous statement on an audio issue…except she's said this before on Twitter. (Another great example of him hiring intelligently yeah?)

15. Trump's wife, Melania Trump apparently lied about her college credentials in her biography at the RNC and on her website. (And when she pulled the inaccurate biography down from her website, she lied again saying it "has been removed because it does not accurately reflect [her] current business and professional interests.") Dad, as you know, I also only did two years of college so that's not the problem. But is there *anything* about these people that stands up to scrutiny?

16. Trump's own website is calling out his supporters to "Help [Him] Stop Crooked Hillary From Rigging This Election!" As he said in Pennsylvania, "The only way we can lose, in my opinion — and I really mean this, Pennsylvania — is if cheating goes on."As Brian Stelter from CNN pointed out, "suggesting an election is going to be stolen? This is third world dictatorship stuff."

17. Chris Frates has pointed out that Trump has been surrounded by immigrants his entire life. Melania Trump, his current wife, is from Slovenia and then there is Ivana, his first wife, who was born in Czechoslovakia. So it sounds like he really only has a problem with a *certain kind* of immigrants.

18. You know I've done my fair share of ghostwriting and how intimate that relationship can get. The writer's job is to see inside the person's soul. Tony Schwartz, the ghostwriter behind Trump's *The Art of the Deal,* decided that he could no longer *not* speak out about what he saw during his time with Trump. I'll leave you his words without comment: "I genuinely believe that if Trump wins and gets the nuclear codes, there is an excellent possibility it will lead to the end of civilization." Oh, and what would he call the book if he were to write it again? "The Sociopath."

19. This isn't a big deal, I know, but I think it's funny that his entrance to the RNC was to the soundtrack of Air Force One.

He knows there is a difference between fake and real presidents right?

20. Maybe he's literally tone deaf? Because Trump announced his running mate, Mike Pence, to the Rolling Stones' "You Can't Always Get What You Want." I thought this guy was a brilliant marketer? I thought he was a masterful manager? Did *anybody think about the subtext of that musical choice?* Ezra Klein, who was equally stumped, wrote in an article about Trump's bizarre introduction of Mike Pence, "What did we all hear, over and over again, as we waited for Trump to introduce Mike Pence, his "first choice from the start!"? 'You can't always get what you want…'" It's a little thing, I know, but it says a lot.

21. Perhaps we can excuse going wildly off message with the understanding that Donald Trump doesn't actually have a message or a campaign to go back to. NBC found that thus far in the general election Donald Trump has spent $0—that is, not a cent—on television advertising so far in the general election. This is a guy who has to win multiple swing states. This is a guy who is now very far behind in the race. Yet he's also a guy who has raised, last month alone, more than $35M from small-dollar donors. If he's not buying ads, *where is the money going?*

22. I also liked this analysis of the email campaigns of Hillary and Donald. Messages aside, Hillary's have all the best practices of modern marketing. They're friendly, they have clear calls to action, they're optimized to raise funds in various amounts. Trump? He sent one underwhelming email in 8 days. His whole appeal as a candidate is that he's supposedly a brilliant marketer and even more brilliant business man. What does it say that she's running circles around him here? Maybe all he's actually good at it is *self-promotion.*

23. In a conversation with Sean Hannity on *Fox News* Trump criticized reporters at the *New York Times* by saying they "don't write good." He delivered that line three times!

24. This was an actual tweet that Trump sent out at the end of July: "Looks to me like the Bernie people will fight. If not, their blood, sweat, and tears was a total waste of time. Kaine stands for the opposite!" We all make typos…but then again, most of us aren't running for president and if we were, we'd probably take the time to check our work. I remember you telling me that you respected George W. Bush's decision to reinstate a strict dress code at the White House, that it was dignified and reflected the office. This guy can't even spell!

25. "I always wanted to get the Purple Heart," Trump told a crowd in Ashburn, Va. after a veteran gave him a copy of his Purple Heart medal. "This was much easier." The Purple Heart is one of this country's most cherished military honors. In describing it the way he did–as someone who wormed their way out of serving in Vietnam and as someone who just insulted a Gold Star Mother–Trump seemed to have no shame in treating the medal like a free sample at the grocery store. It was a despicable comment and an insult to the many Purple Heart veterans who earned the honor by their blood.

26. Last week Politico reported that 70 Republicans have signed a letter to Reince Priebus, the Republican National Committee Chairman, to cut off any funding for Donald Trump. And as one *New York Times* story reported, the advisers surrounding him "now increasingly concede that Mr. Trump may be beyond coaching;"

27. A poll recently showed that African Americans were polling 99-1% for Hillary over Trump. What does that say? When an *entire race* of voters see you as a threat (13 percent of the population of the United States), maybe we should try to understand why that is? Are they the canary in the coal mine?

28. I read an interesting piece by Harlan Coben that speculated as to why Donald Trump goes off script so often. He thrives on the reactions from the crowd. The audience starts to drift? He says something shocking. The shocking thing stops being so shocking? He takes it up a notch. It makes a lot of sense—and I've caught myself doing it in talks before. It's scary up there, and that behavior takes some of the edge off. Here's the thing: The President is supposed to be OK with scary situations. They need to be secure enough in themselves and in standing alone that they don't endlessly pander to the crowd. Nero needed the Roman people to shower him with applause, Commodus needed the Coliseum's rapt attention. We need someone who can bravely do the right thing, who can listen while others speak, who can *not* indulge every impulse. Yet despite every incentive to hold it together—to just *appear* presidential—Trump doesn't seem to be able to.

29. You're a Republican so Trump's petulant refusal to support other Republicans matters. He initially refused to support Paul Ryan because he wasn't seeing enough "strong leadership" and he claimed that he was withholding support because John McCain *didn't support veterans*. It's hard to even respond to these things seriously—but Trump was the guy who claimed that McCain *wasn't a war hero because he'd been captured and taken prisoner,* right? These are the people he's supposed to be able to work with in order to pass legislation. Does he have any allies at this point? He might actually have to fix it "alone" because he's pissed off every single person who has tried to support him despite all the reasons not to.

30. What does it say that Ted Cruz declined to endorse Trump at the convention? "I am not in the habit of supporting people who attack my wife and attack my father," he said. His refusal to endorse Trump is not surprising given that during his speech he said that "We deserve leaders who stand for principle, unite us all behind shared values, cast aside anger for love. That is the standard we should expect, from everybody."

31. There was Donald Trump's casual remark about not stepping in to defend fellow NATO countries, saying he would do only if they'd "fulfilled their obligations to us." That is, he'd only do it they'd *paid* for our protection. I thought we'd learned with your father and with your father's father, the price that Americans have to pay when European countries are allowed acts of wanton aggression and invasion (that is…we have to go over there and fight and die in even great number).

32. Stoking a false claim that the US had exchanged cash for hostages from Iran, Trump claimed that he actually saw footage of a plane unloading millions in cash. Turns out, he was just watching TV and had no idea what he was talking about. Apparently, this was the *one thing,* Trump felt he was objectively mistaken enough to admit he was wrong about. Trump admitted on Twitter: "The plane I saw on television was the hostage plane in Geneva, Switzerland, not the plane carrying $400 million in cash going to Iran!" But on John McCain, on mocking a disabled reporter, on the plagiarism, on the Khan family? Nope.

33. What should one think when the former head of the CIA accuses Trump of becoming "an unwitting agent of the Russian Federation?" What he means is that Putin has manipulated Donald and played on his vulnerabilities throughout his campaign, making him in a sense, an asset to the very enemy that Mitt Romney spent most of his campaign criticizing Obama for not taking seriously enough.

34. Trump's speech at the Republican Convention contained this statement: "Nobody knows the system better than me, which is why I alone can fix it. I alone can fix it." We talked a lot about ego when I was writing my last book and I think in a different context, we both would have laughed at a remark like this as being absurd and delusional. And that doesn't even get into the fact that our entire system of government is designed to prevent the President from fixing things "alone." In fact, we have a name for people who try to do that: *fascists*.

35. One of the strongest arguments for a conservative to vote for Trump despite all the problems they might have is that next President is likely to have incredible influence via the next few Supreme Court appointments. The argument is that whatever you think of Trump, it's important that Republicans be able to name solid judges to the Supreme Court. But why are you so sure he'd do a good job? Because he says he would? Look at this video of Trump directly contradicting himself on dozens and dozens of issues. Look at his track record on hiring and vetting people. Look at how he chose a VP, hemming and hawing and consulting his children for the final choice. *That's who you want appointing people to serve for life, that's who you want picking the people who ultimately judge our laws at the highest level?*

36. Even though the Trump campaign had hired two high-powered speechwriters for Melania's speech at the Republican Convention, she and Trump decided to override their advice and work with someone in-house—someone that Trump had personally hired. Of course, we know how that went. The speechwriter was incompetent and allowed a largely plagiarized section—plagiarized from Michelle Obama's own speech addressing her convention no less—to be read to millions and millions of people.

37. Stuff happens, obviously, and as I learned from you, it's what *leaders do when stuff happens* that matters. What did Trump's team do? First, they denied it and tried to spin it as not plagiarism because it was all common phrases. Then Trump claimed all press is good press." Then Trump declined to fire the writer or hold anyone accountable for what happened. He let the speechwriter apologize—but of course, as the guy in charge, he refused to take responsibility for any of it himself.

38. At his first intelligence briefing, Trump is bringing with him Lt. Gen. Michael Flynn, who in Garry Kasparov's words is "someone who openly works with Putin's propaganda channel Russia Today." Flynn also got to casually sit next to Putin last December at a dinner in Moscow. (He also had a paid speaking gig while in Russia as well.)

39. At a rally in Florida, Trump pulled out a graphic and showed it on stage. Not a big deal. Except that *David Duke,* the white supremacist and former Ku Klux Klan leader, *is fond of using the exact same graphic.*

40. Another funny thing about that graphic. Remember when Donald Trump got in trouble for using that Star of David over a picture of Hillary Clinton? A lot of people said it was anti-Semitic. Of course, he denied that was his intention. Well, that David Duke graphic used in Florida? It's got another one on it. This time with Hillary Clinton on a $20 bill.

41. And a third thing about David Duke. In an interview with NPR, he said something about Donald Trump voters: We've already polled inside the Trump voters, and we know that we're going to carry 75 to 80 percent of those who are going to vote for Trump." The host asked, "You think Trump voters are your voters?" His response? *"Well, of course they are!"*

42. According to *The Atlantic*, Trump also appears to be laying out a strategy to skip the presidential debates—which of course, just like the election, Hillary & the Dems are trying to rig," as he said in a tweet.

43. Much has been made of Hillary's association with unsavory characters. I agree, it's alarming. Her continued support of Debbie Wasserman Schultz, that so and so apparently appeared at one of her rallies. These are legitimate issues. Trump tried to call Hillary out on this recently …without grasping the irony (to say nothing of the incredible hypocrisy) in Florida when he attacked Hillary for allowing the father of the Orlando shooter to sit in the stands behind her, yet beside Trump, in a reserved seat, sat Mark Foley, an ex-congressman who resigned in disgrace in 2006 after sending sexually explicit messages to under-age teenage boys."

44. That's the other thing about Trump. Hillary is one of the least popular candidates in history, but by a large margin she is not the least popular candidate *in this election.* Because of who Trump is, because of his inability to do even the most basic things required of a candidate, Hillary has been allowed to skate on many, many issues that the media should be grilling her over. How would this trend play out if Trump were elected? Would he suck the air out of the room in every debate, during every issue and make himself the center of attention in every crisis? Is this going to help us have the tough conversations I know you know we need to have as a country?

45. Trump has claimed that the media is aligned against him. He's accused the *New York Times* of being a "failing" paper and called *CNN* "disgusting." He's even banned sites like *Politico* and *BuzzFeed* from his rallies. This attitude reminds me a lot of something. In one of Nixon's famous rants, he said "The press is the enemy. Write that on a blackboard 100 times and never forget it." I've said a lot of things about the media in my writings, but I understand that a free and open press is essential to our democracy. As a marketer, I also understand that if you live by the sword, you die by the sword. One calculation estimates that Trump got nearly $3 *billion* dollars worth of free media in the early stages of the election. Was he complaining then? Besides, I thought he said that all press is good press?

46. Donald Trump has said so much ridiculous and flat out incorrect things that the media has had to devise new ways of correcting him with on-air graphics in the course of their endless coverage of every remark and event. Some examples: "Trump says he watched (nonexistent) video of Iran receiving cash." "Trump: I never said Japan should have nukes (he did)", "Trump's son: "Father apologized to Khans (he hasn't)"

47. Transcribers of his speeches have also complained how long it takes due to his confusing, manic and often unintelligible syntax. They sometimes have to use teams of people just to get it right. As one transcriber put it, Almost every time we have done a transcript of him there is something in there that makes you wonder what is going on." What they mean is that he is often deliberately obtuse—he says things in a way that allows him to pretend he means one thing while signaling to another group. In other cases, what he says makes so little sense, they wonder what on earth he was talking about ("word salad" is the phrase). All of which is an issue considering it's the president's job to effectively communicate to every citizen of this country as well as have productive, clear and coherent discussions with international leaders and allies.

48. I've given you a lot of things Trump has done, but notice what he *hasn't* done? The things a candidate is supposed to do. He hasn't articulated his policies. He hasn't shown that he has even the slightest grasp on what the job of being president would entail. He hasn't released his tax returns. He hasn't told us, in any detail, who he would be listening to and who would be advising him—other than, of course, himself.

49. When I published the first letter, I was on my way to London and then to Germany. You would be shocked at the reactions from people in other countries. They're incredulous that we're even thinking about this. The *Washington Post* wrote that US citizens traveling abroad are finding themselves on an "apology tour" trying to explain what is going on here—I felt that for sure. More than that, I remember a morning on my trip to Berlin, going on an early morning run past the Reichstag. The building is pocked with bullet holes and in the corner is a memorial (only recently erected) to the legislators that were murdered as Hitler consolidated power. It was a reminder to me of the stakes here—that even if there is a 1% chance of something like that happening, even all the warning signs are overblown, that we have a duty to stop it before it happens. It's worth considering the courage—and listening—to the conservatives who have broken with their party over Donald Trump. Even if you disagree with them, even if these protests turn out to be overblown, that takes real courage. I think we should follow their lead.

I know I've gone on way too long here so I'll wrap up.

The final thing about Trump is this: No one has been subjected to more criticism and made more stumbles in a campaign than he has. It's completely unprecedented. In the last fourteen months, have you seen a single instance in which he seems to have learned from any of it? Have you seen a single adjustment or improvement along the way? Has there been even one incident where you've seen him—when subjected to an overwhelming public response or media backlash—stop and go "You know what, I was wrong. Here's my explanation and apology and in the future I will be different." Have you seen that even one time? Insulting a Gold Star Mother, calling on a foreign power to intervene in an election, urging violence against his opponent, attacking a war hero, using anti-Semitic materials…all of those would have been easy opportunities for a mea culpa and an adjustment. Yet there were none.

So why should we think that as President he is going to have that skill? It's the steepest learning curve of any job in the world. It will inevitably be filled with mistakes and errors and problems. If he's not accountable to feedback or criticism now—at the time he is most in need of public support and approval—why the hell would he be any different on the day he takes office?

People don't change, you told me. Actions speak louder than words. I think, in this case, that's the best advice you've ever given me.

Please Dad, for all these reasons and so many more, don't vote for Donald Trump.

PART 4

Donald Trump was fighting to regain the momentum from Hillary Clinton after his below-average performance in the first Presidential Debate. On October 9th, however, the release of archived footage from NBC showed him making disparaging remarks about women in conversation with Billy Bush, saying that he just "grabbed them and started kissing them" and that he "grabbed them by the pussy."

After denying that he ever assaulted any woman during the second Presidential Debate, multiple women came forward to claim that they had been sexually assaulted by Donald Trump. Trump claimed that all they women were liars.

His remarks were a firestorm in the national media, and our contributors had a lot to say about them too. For the next few weeks, we would receive countless submissions from both men and women who discussed the deeply personal issues of sexual assault.

20

Donald Trump, Locker Room Banter Is Not An Excuse To Justify Saying You Can 'Grab Me By My Pussy'

Ari Eastman

In my latest poetry book, I have a poem called "Boys Will Be Boys." Now, it's a fairly tame incident. In it, a boy and I get in trouble in class for doing something dumb (we cut a stand of our friend's hair, sorry Briana!) and are sent to the principal. It's elementary school and it's not as if we get in big trouble. But the point of the poem is that we're treated differently in the office. This behavior is *expected* of him. After all, boys will be boys. They just can't help themselves!

But that's not the case for me. I should have known better. I was a young lady. A girl. I don't get to make excuses.

This 'boys will be boys' mentality continues as our boys age. And it gets more and more toxic. It ages with them, becomes more dangerous to women, and to them as well. **This rigid idea of masculinity, of making excuses because men just can't help themselves, hurts EVERYBODY (including men).** It robs men of dimensions and makes them appear as nothing more than Neanderthals, these Things That Can't Control What They Do. It then turns women into potential survivors who should always stay vigilant. It's why women travel in groups, go to the bathroom together. Or why today, when I thought about going out to eat by myself (something I love to do) and a man cat-called me on my way, I decided it was better to be safe and just went home. That's not okay.

Degrading women is not "just what boys do."

Or, it damn sure shouldn't be. I don't want to hear that that's how you talk with your buddies. Stop. Don't do that. Degrading anyone is unacceptable.

"Locker room banter"—as Trump says—is us ALLOWING behavior to be okay. It's us saying, "They don't mean it!" when they absolutely do. You don't just say things you don't mean. There's usually truth behind jokes. When people are speaking candidly in private, they are exposing who they really are. And what they think. That's them at their rawest.

We have to be better than this. **We have to hold our children accountable, regardless of their gender.** We have to teach consent. My god, we have to teach consent.

And PLEASE don't tell your boys, "What if it was your mother? sister? daughter?"

Instead, say, "This is a human being you are talking about."

Rape culture starts slowly and in the smallest ways. But it grows bigger. And when we tell our boys it's okay, we turn them into men who say things like, "Just grab 'em by the pussy."

21

27 Things People ACTUALLY Talk About In Locker Rooms (Spoiler: It's Not Sexual Assault)

Kendra Syrdal

1. "Do you have a spare tampon?"

2. "Hey FYI that shower's totally out of hot water."

3. "JFC that class kicked my ass."

4. "I'm going to demolish a burger after that workout."

5. *total silence because everyone's on their phones post getting rocked at Andrew's 5:30 spin class*

6. "Excuse me," *shuffles by Caroline who's putting her hair up to get to your own locker*

7. "Where'd you get those yoga pants?"

8. "Smoothies?"

9. "Holy shit I'm going to be so sore tomorrow."

10. "Can I borrow your shampoo? I left mine at home."

11. "Ughhhh I'm running so late I have to change in 30 seconds or I'm going to miss class."

12. "Dammit, I forgot deodorant. Sorry to whoever is next to me."

13. "I can't believe that dude didn't wipe down the machine when he was done. So gross…"

14. "Are you taking the weekend off or are you coming tomorrow?"

15. "Oh my god I can't wait until it's nice out again so I can go running outside."

16. "How do you feel about that new instructor? I'm on the fence."

17. *more silence because everyone is just getting changed in peace*

18. "Hey! How was your week?"

19. "Can you spot me?"

20. "I definitely should've eaten before that yoga class. I feel like I'm going to pass out."

21. "Pardon me," *said as you scoot in to use the mirror to redo your make up or redo your hair*

22. "Are we still on for drinks tomorrow?"

23. "Do I have your number? Here, put it in my phone so I can text you the address."

24. "Can I borrow your foam roller?"

25. "That felt so good. I feel so strong right now."

26. "Same time tomorrow?"

27. "Did you see the debates? Donald Trump makes me literally scream at my TV…"

Dear Donald Trump: If You Actually Had 'More Respect For Women Than Anyone' You'd Do These 12 Things

Kim Quindlen

1. You would treat every woman you know like your equal because that's exactly what she is.

2. You would realize that a woman's worth has *ABSOLUTELY NOTHING* to do with her looks, her weight, her style, and anything else related to her physical appearance.

3. And not only would you realize this, but you would *act* like it. Your actions toward women – your respect towards them, your behavior towards them, your words towards them

– would reflect the fact that you understand that their worth and their dignity are not derived from their looks.

4. You would know that words you've used in the past to describe women, including *fat pigs, dogs, slobs,* and *disgusting animals* are never and should never be acceptable in any capacity whatsoever.

5. You would remember, *every* time you speak, that millions of young women around the country and around the world are hearing your words, hearing how other people react to them and what other people think is okay when it comes to how women are treated.

6. And you would remember, *every* time you speak, that millions of young *men* around the country and around the world are also hearing your words, and are learning what you think is apparently an acceptable way to speak to and treat women.

7. You would understand that 'locker room talk' is not normal, is not okay, and is not excusable.

8. You would understand that your version of 'locker room talk' perpetuates rape culture and that it's so much more harmful than you've been currently playing it off to be.

9. You would understand that a woman is meant to stand next to you, not behind you.

10. You would speak to your current political opponent only about *her* decisions and *her* actions, instead of constantly bringing up past actions and mistakes made by her husband.

You would remember that *she* is the one running for president, not him.

11. And during your debates with her, you would refrain from interrupting her–dozens and dozens of times–the same way she shows you respect by not interrupting you.

12. You would understand that women are not here on this earth for YOU. They are not here for your entertainment, they are not here for you to look at, they are not here for your sexual pleasure, they are not here to stand next to you as a pretty ornament, they are not here to be a side character in your story. Women are their own protagonists, they are their own bosses, and they have dignity and worth regardless of what you think of them. And if you were smart, you'd realize that you need women a hell of a lot more than they need you.

23

This Is What It's Like Dating Someone Who Supports Donald Trump

Kelli Rose

I suppose I should start off by saying that my (long time) boyfriend is one of the best people I have ever met, and I trust him with 100% of my life—**or at least I thought so until this current presidential election began.**

He is older than me, being 16 years my senior. We grew up during completely different generations, and his political views make that extremely evident. Like so many other fellow millennials, I guess you could say I am very left wing. I am pro-choice and in strong support of Planned Parenthood and all of the good that they do for our female community with the services that they provide; I want full equality for women, including income and job eligibility equality; I am a strong ally to the

LGBTQ community; I believe in gun control and more extensive background checks; and I support universal health care. I have six children, five of them being girls. It would be an understatement to say that I am terrified of *all* of them growing up in a country where they may not have the same opportunities or privileges as others, depending on their gender or sexual preference, whatever that may turn out to be. **All I truly want is a country where they feel (and are) accepted and can thrive to their full potential.**

Call me naïve, but when my boyfriend and I started dating and decided to begin our life together by starting a family, our specific political views were not on my mind. He was (and still is) so good to me, and he has treated me with more respect than any man I have ever dated. I knew that he was traditional and wanted to provide for our family and didn't expect me to work but being the independent woman that I am, I prefer to be in the workforce just as much as he is. It has only been when I was with child that I admitted defeat (that's exactly what it felt like) and decided to quit to stay at home when my health and that of my unborn babies could no longer tolerate it.

He knew that I was full of girl power and loved the gays and respected my opinions on those matters. Once the presidential election was in full force, that's when I learned how much he was more against me and those that I support than he was for us.

I can live with the fact that he doesn't want stricter gun laws. Granted, he's a Southern man from a small town in Mississippi. I can live with the fact that he doesn't trust Hillary Clinton as president because she clearly cannot be trusted and has completely changed her views on *everything* since beginning this presidential election. I also understand that the *email situation* and investigation has lost the trust of many.

What I *cannot* live with is the fact that he stands behind a man that has no respect for women, the LGBTQ community, other races and other religions. How can you support a man that talks about women like they are mere objects that can be used and tossed away for their own selfish gain? You can call it "locker room talk" if you'd like, but it is sexual assault when there is no consent. *Get real.* He bashes Hillary for representing a rapist in court, but he *actually* made a remark that only a rapist himself would say, so what does that tell you about the man that you're putting your daughters' rights (and futures) into his hands? How can you stand behind a man that thinks that races or religions other than his own can cause a person to be disposable and not deserve the same treatment and opportunities as he does?

I try my best to not judge others on their political views because what's the point in trying to convince someone why they should change their minds when they're clearly blinded by what they want to see? (I suppose those against my views would say the same about me, as well.) I bite my tongue on Facebook and only share my views through funny, passive-aggressive memes to keep the mood light and refrain from starting a feud with Facebook keyboard gangsters. (We've all got 'em on our friends list, and you know it.) *To each their own.* But it is terrifying knowing that the man that I love and the father of my children, supports a man that will not support us. I have spent hours upon hours trying to open his eyes and his heart to the seriousness of the situation to no avail.

What's going to happen to *us* if Trump wins this election? This is a real fear that I have, and *you should, too.* To have someone that wants to rule with such hate towards others is not the way to make this country great again. We need someone that loves and supports every American and wants us all to thrive in a country that was based on freedom and opportunity. They say that we millennials get offended too easily but all we truly want is true equality and security for everyone alike. I don't see the harm in wanting our neighbor to feel as safe and welcome as we are supposed to feel in the Land of the Free. If loving my neighbor, myself and my children is wrong, then I don't want to be right.

24

Donald Trump Doesn't Know How To Spell 'Wikileaks'

Jacob Geers

Much ado has been made in the media about Julian Assange's "Wikileaks" organization, which has been slowly releasing the private emails of Hillary Clinton campaign Chairman John Podesta.

While many of the emails have been embarrassing, revealing the extent to which Hillary Clinton's image is crafted and carefully controlled by staffers (who guessed), none of the emails yet have been truly damning—despite attempts from the Trump campaign to take several out of context.

Donald Trump thinks that the media should be talking more about these leaks, however. He thinks that CNN, MSNBC, Fox News, ABC should stop talking about the women who are accusing him of sexual assault and start talking about the fact that the Hillary Clinton campaign is indeed, political and played politics.

He has tweeted about "Wikileaks" quite a bit. Well, at least, he has tweeted about something *close* to "Wikileaks."

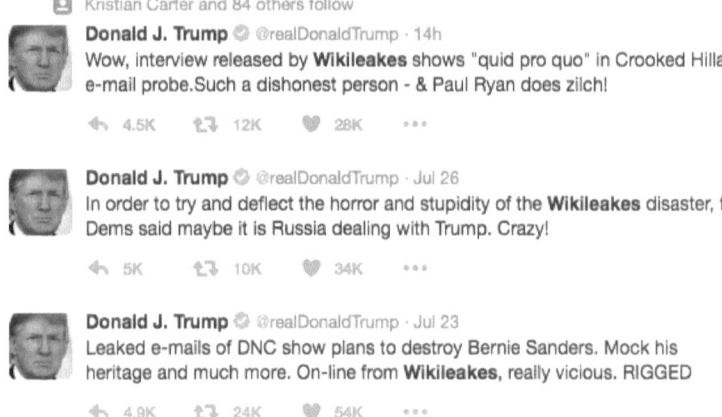

Twitter / Donald J. Trump

In these three instances—over the course of four months—Donald Trump has tweeted about *"Wikileakes"* which is not an organization, or a word of any kind. These tweets have received a combined 46,000 retweets, with potentially countless impressions across Twitter.

The misspelling features the (not) word "leakes" instead of "leaks." Perhaps Donald Trump was thinking of entertainment personality NeNe Leakes?

And to be fair, Donald Trump has managed to spell the organization "Wikileaks" correctly in four instances on Twitter.

4 / 7: that's a majority, right?

Donald J. Trump @realDonaldTrump · 20h
We've all wondered how Hillary avoided prosecution for her email scheme. **Wikileaks** may have found the answer. Obama!

Podesta Leaks: The Obama-Clinton E-mails, by An...
Among the most noteworthy of the hacked e-mails from John Podesta's accounts is an exchange in which Podesta consults Clinton consigliere Cheryl Mills abo...
nationalreview.com

↩ 4.7K   ↻ 20K   ♥ 32K   ···

Donald J. Trump @realDonaldTrump · Oct 12
Very little pick-up by the dishonest media of incredible information provided by **WikiLeaks**. So dishonest! Rigged system!

↩ 9.9K   ↻ 21K   ♥ 54K   ···

Donald J. Trump @realDonaldTrump · Oct 11
I hope people are looking at the disgraceful behavior of Hillary Clinton as exposed by **WikiLeaks**. She is unfit to run.

↩ 11K   ↻ 24K   ♥ 58K   ···

Donald J. Trump @realDonaldTrump · Jul 23
The **Wikileaks** e-mail release today was so bad to Sanders that it will make it impossible for him to support her, unless he is a fraud!

↩ 3.6K   ↻ 15K   ♥ 37K   ···

Twitter / Donald J. Trump

Okay, okay, we all make spelling mistakes now and again. Just the other day I spelled a relatively common fashion item incorrectly throughout an article. But I'm not running for President, or trying to convince people that the elections are a sham because the *world is rigged against me.*

If you are so brilliant that the entire establishment of planet Earth is trying to take you down, you should probably know how to spell the organization that you're gleefully cheering on for trashing your opponent.

25

The Biggest Problem With The 2016 Election Is The Dismissal Of Trump's Sexism

Alyssa Lynn

The Presidential election has brought out a whole lot of ugly these past few months. You're considered evil if you like either candidate, dividing people throughout the United States. Whether you want to vote for Hilary Clinton or Donald Trump is your business. If you believe one candidate will help this country more than the other that you have every right to make that choice for yourself. This isn't an article about which candidate would make a better President.

I believe that the larger issue at hand is the dismissal of Donald Trump's behavior.

The bigger problem is the excuses made that attempt to lessen the severity of the intentionally offensive and vulgar language that is Donald Trump's natural and organic self.

Donald Trump has exhibited sexist and racist behavior and is unable to take responsibility for any of his actions. He constantly blames others, playing the victim. Trump has claimed media bias in favor of Hillary Clinton. He is absolutely right, there *is* media bias against him.

But when you are proud of the fact that you can grab any woman by the pussy because you are a "celebrity" you don't leave the media with many choices.

There isn't a positive way to spin that. Donald Trump has repeatedly tried to associate behavior of Bill Clinton with Hilary Clinton, although they are two different people. Yet ,he does not want us to associate his past behavior with him, the same person. That doesn't make much sense to me.

This isn't the first time Donald Trump has shown what little respect he holds for women. You can Google hundred of quotes that Donald Trump has made over the years. Although the media is painting him as this volatile and irrational jerk, they are just using the material he has given. Unable to deal with the reality he has created, he attacks others with offensive and hurtful words. Fat, ugly, pig, gross, flat chested, clown, neurotic, a mess, lazy, slob, dog, and unattractive. These are words he uses regularly.

Michelle Obama said it best, **"This is not normal."**

What is scariest about the dismissal of such behavior?

Those who are humored by Donald Trump's words and explain this is who he is and they have no problem with that.

This dismissive behavior is the same behavior that allowed Brock Turner to do three months in jail for raping an unconscious woman behind a dumpster. This is the same behavior that claims if a woman is drunk enough and/or showing enough skin, she is asking for it. No matter how many times she says no, she wants it.

Sexism is alive today and the behavior of Donald Trump is not something that should be ignored. This is happening, right here right now. These are real problems and ignoring them is inexcusable. Overlooking this sort of behavior inevitably allows it to continue.

26

Trump Should Read This Moving Note President George HW Bush Wrote Bill Clinton After Losing

Jacob Geers

In last night's Presidential Debate, Republican nominee Donald J. Trump refused to say whether he would accept the results of the election (assuming he loses).

His statement is shocking and pretty much unprecedented in United States politics. Our tradition of democracy has allowed for the peaceful transition of power across parties dozens upon dozens of times—including in the year 1992.

In the 1992 election, incumbent President George H.W. Bush lost his bid for re-election to President Bill Clinton. President Bush, did not, however, throw a tantrum or refuse to accept the result. He respected the voters' decision and wrote this heartfelt note to the man who bested him.

Dear Bill,

When I walked into this office just now I felt the same sense of wonder and respect that I felt four years ago. I know you will feel that, too.

I wish you great happiness here. I never felt the loneliness some Presidents have described.

There will be very tough times, made even more difficult by criticism you may not think is fair. I'm not a very good one to give advice; but just don't let the critics discourage you or push you off course.

You will be our President when you read this note. I wish you well. I wish your family well.

Your success is now our country's success. I am rooting for you.

Good luck,

George

This gracious note does not signal bitterness or resentment at his loss. It shows integrity and honor from a man who respects democracy more than he cares about his personal success.

Donald J. Trump would do well to look at President George H.W. Bush as a model.

27

For All The Fathers Who Are Voting For Donald Trump

Sydney White

Jennifer Conti, an OB-GYN and medical journalist, recently wrote an article about her experience this election season for Slate. The article, "A Conversation Between and OB-GYN and Her Trump-Supporting Father About Sexual Assault" throws into sharp relief a dichotomy many women in America are struggling with this election cycle. For many women, like Conti, it boils down to this: My father is a good man who loves, defends, and champions me, but he is willing to vote for someone who, at the very least, believes sexual assault like what I have experienced is perfectly acceptable.

At worst, my father is willing to cast his vote for a man who has assaulted women in the same way I have been assaulted. At worst, my father is complicit in my assault. It's a damn tough pill to swallow.

I am lucky. I do not have to ask these questions about my father. This November he's casting his vote for Hillary Clinton. Every day on Facebook I can watch him advocate for women in the comments sections of his friends' posts and shared links. For my father, I am not a special snowflake possessing a special social status by virtue of my relationship with him. My personhood is not to be respected because "I am his daughter" but because I am a woman like every other: deserving of respect, decency, and bodily autonomy.

That is not the case for many women. Many women struggle with fathers who love them, would fight fiercely for their rights to their bodies but would abandon women as a whole. Conti is one of those women. Her father chased the man who assaulted her through a toy store but, simultaneously, her father will champion her assailant when he casts his ballot for Trump in November. Conti isn't alone. On my father's Facebook, I watch men with daughters defend Trump's statements as locker room talk. I watch them refuse to accept the old maxim: Thoughts lead to words. Words lead to actions. Actions lead to character.

I would like to be very clear, a man who says, "When you're a star they let you do it. You can do anything. Grab them by the pussy. You can do anything" is a man who assaults women. He knows he can "do anything" because he has. It isn't like saying, "I might be able to get away with something but am not completely sure because I would never try it." The statement is, "You can do anything." I, Donald Trump, can do anything.

A man who says, "When you're a star they let you do it. You can do anything. Grab them by the pussy" is a man who believes his status and influence entitles him to the bodies of women, at will, without their consent. "I don't even wait" he bragged to Billy Bush. He doesn't wait for what? Consent. Don't wait for consent, "just kiss" and grab them by the pussy.

Fathers, when you cast a vote for Donald Trump when you defend him online or in your homes, you tell your daughters that their safety and agency can be sacrificed, by you, on the altar of your economic or social preferences.

You tell them that the sexual assault of women is a small price to pay for lower taxes and fewer immigrants. You tell them their bodies are their own until it is politically expedient for you. You remind them they are always unsafe, even in their own homes. Is that true?

Is it true that in your anger about Hillary Clinton, immigration, taxes, and the war in Iraq, you would offer up your daughter's pussy to Donald Trump and men like him? Men have been buying status, power, and position with women's bodies as currency for millennia; perhaps 2016 is no different.

Don't say, "It was locker room talk." Or words don't mean he actually did it. Or it was 11 years ago. Or it was lighthearted joking between men. You can, and maybe should, read a plethora of articles online about how these excuses are completely insufficient, and I don't seek to rehash those explanations here. It wasn't "locker room talk" because that conception of locker room talk does not exist. It was a description of assault.

Words have power and meaning, especially for a President of the United States. Obama once said his words move markets. **A President's words change the world.** Sexually assaulting someone is not a joke, witty banter, or an amusing anecdote. Don't say, "but Bill Clinton," because Bill Clinton is not on the ballot. He is not running for President. His actions are his, and his alone; they are not relevant to any discussion about this year's Presidential Nominees. Those issues and concerns have their place but, like Bill Clinton, they are not on the ballot or in the voting booth.

One in five women on college campuses is sexually assaulted; some estimates place the numbers even higher. I want to tell you what that feels like to live with, so you know. I want you to know what that feels like so when your daughter comes to you and asks you about Donald Trump, or tells you about her assault, or her fears, you might understand better where she comes from.

The first time a man asked me to perform oral sex on him, I was 10 years old and in 5th grade. He was a family friend and watching my siblings and me while my parents were out. He offered toys and gifts. When I hid between the chair and ottoman in our living room he begged me not to tell anyone what he had said. I remember the pit in my stomach, cowering behind the ottoman, pulling it towards me so I would be squeezed a little tighter between the ottoman and the chair. If I could just wedge myself in tight enough, if I could be small enough, I would be safe. I remember crouching stock-still, par- alyzed with fear and unable to speak. I remember closing my eyes, wishing this wasn't happening, begging it not to be real. Eventually, he gave up trying to convince me and left me alone. I ran upstairs, locked my door, and hide in the closet until morning. I was 10 years old. I never told my parents. He told me no one would believe me.

Three years later, I was assaulted on a church youth mission trip. I was 13 years old, just about to enter high school, one month shy of my 14th birthday. On the pretext of exploring a tree house near our campsite, a 17-year-old boy cornered me alone. He reached under my shirt and grabbed my breast. The fear and paralysis were so familiar: stock-still, unable to speak, unable to move. I was 13 years old, 3,000 miles from home, with a group of chaperons I didn't know well, trying to make friends so I wouldn't go into high school alone. After what seemed like hours, he took his hand away and climbed down from the tree house.

He cornered and assaulted me several more times on the trip. I remember we had to fill out this chart. It asked for personal information for everyone on the trip, things like favorite song, favorite sports team, favorite subject, etc. It was designed so everyone could get to know each other one-on-one. There was a ritual public shaming if you failed to do so. Each person without a completed sheet would be forced to stand in the middle of a circle and sing and dance for their supper and the amusement of their peers. He used that sheet of questions as a pretext to get me alone, despite my attempts to avoid him. Telling other people in the group that he was going to work on it with me. Once he trapped me in the corner of a stairwell, kissed me, reached into my jeans, and grabbed my crotch. Once, he snuck into the kitchen when I was alone prepping lunches for the day and grabbed my breasts.

I was 13 years old, on a church mission trip. He was 17, about to be a senior in high school. He was the son of my sister's third-grade teacher. He was a star athlete on multiple varsity teams. A few months later, after school had started, he showed up on my bus. He told me he learned I was on his route, and didn't drive that day so he could sit with me. He sat down next to me, trapping me between him and the window, so I couldn't get away. My heart was pounding a deep dread welled in the pit of my stomach. My hands, arms, and legs were shaking. I told him never to touch me again, stood up, pushed past him, and sat somewhere else.

It takes longer than you think to find your voice when someone is violating you. For a while you sit there in shock, unable to believe or comprehend that the unthinkable is happening. I found my voice the 5th time he tried to put his hands on me. At first, I was ashamed. Ashamed I didn't say anything sooner, ashamed of the paralysis and fear I felt, ashamed I let it happen. I'm not anymore. I was 13 years old, surrounded by strangers, and terrified. I did nothing wrong. He should bear that shame, not me. He was 4 years older than me; he assaulted me. I saw him at family parties for years afterward, and I never went back to youth group.

I was lucky. Through high school and college it was pretty smooth sailing, the normal little violations women live with, but nothing paralyzing. Nothing I couldn't handle. (Think about that phrase for a moment. Think about what it means to have to learn to cope with sexual assault on a daily basis such that you have a skill set ready to deploy by age 14.)

Men picking me up around the waist and carrying me around the campus over their shoulders without my permission, as I squirm and beg to be put down. Men throwing erasers, wadded up paper, peanuts, and whatever-the-hell-else they could find down the front of my t-shirt. Men on my swim team asking for my bra size, and taking votes within the team when I refuse to say. Or snapping my bra straps or the straps of my swimsuit. I am grateful every day for a swim coach who put a stop to that right quick.

Men who yell at me out of car windows as I walk home from work. My personal favorite was the car that circled round the block twice, so when they came back they could throw cheap dog toys and dog treats at me. Get it? Because I'm a bitch?

Men at work who ask for my help looking for something, only to follow me around the entire facility staring at my ass. Men call my name to get my attention and then gesture to their crotches. Men who ask my boss if I can be let off work early to go home with them. God, it's just exhausting now. Even the listing is exhausting.

And for all this, I consider myself so lucky. I remember vividly talking with a roommate after our mutual acquaintance was raped. She had reached out to us knowing we were ready, ready with the resources and support she wanted and needed. We were ready because as a woman, you prepare to get raped so you will be ready when it happen to you or someone you love.

We sat there, in our dorm room, and my roommate turned to me and said, "One in five women. When I count the women in my life, just my sisters and I make three. And I hope to God it isn't them. I would rather it be me. At least I know I would be ok."

"I know. Me too," I replied.

Ask yourself what it must feel like to take stock of your friends, sisters, and acquaintances, to count them out, knowing one in five of those women will be sexually assaulted. Imagine what it must feel like to never wish that violation upon any of them, and to instead hope you are the statistic. To hope you are the one in five assaulted or raped, because then your sisters, cousins, nieces, and friends might be spared. Imagine the weight of what it feels like to say, "I would rather it be me."

Imagine carrying it every day. Imagine carrying it down every street you walk, on every train, in every cab, in every work meeting and copy room, every night out at a bar or movie theatre or concert or parade. Imagine carrying it even when you are alone with a man you thought you could trust. Imagine carrying it in your classroom, in your house of worship, in the home you live in.

I am no different from your own daughter. I grew up in a nice suburban neighborhood in the Midwest. I went to a good high school, took honors classes. I studied karate for 10 years and was selected for a traveling team. I have two loving parents and a whole host of other adults who would absolutely without question support me. I have friends who love and support me. I got into a good college and was so excited to go. There is nothing special about me or my story. It could belong to anyone and does belong to so many women. I am not a special snowflake.

When your daughter asks you not to vote for Trump, when she expresses concern and fear over his statements about women, it is because her story is like mine. It is because, like me, she fears powerful, entitled, unapologetic men and for good reason. Your vote for Trump is a vote for a world in which women's safety and security are secondary to your economic and political preferences. Like Conti, I ask the following of you: Please don't vote for Donald Trump. Don't vote, or vote third party, if you cannot bring yourself to vote for Hillary. But do not vote for Donald Trump.

If you are determined to cast your ballot in his name this November, I cannot stop you. But do not vote for him ignorant of the message you send. Do not vote Donald Trump ignorant of your daughter's life story, her experiences and her pain.

She may be a special snowflake to you, to be loved, respected, and cherished. But as much as I wish it were different, to so many men she is just an object for consumption and gratification. For you, your daughter is special. For the rest of the world, she is a woman. Stand with her against people who would try to take her agency from her, against men who assault and harass her.

Imagine your father tells you he loves you, and with the same breath, votes to elect a man who would violate you, allow others to violate you and permit a world where your pain is a punchline in the locker room. Imagine your body is currency to be exchanged, your sexuality an object used to buy a tax plan or immigration reform. A daughter's safety, agency, and bodily autonomy are not prices to be paid by her father for his political agenda. Would you use your daughter to buy yours?

28

Dear President Obama...Please Stay

Daniel Hayes

Mr. President, I watched the third and final Presidential debate last night and I think I want to die. I can't remember ever seeing two worse candidates for President in my lifetime. I honestly can't think of any from before I was born either. I've had to drink my way through all three of these debates (and most of October) and I know I'm not alone.

Look, I freely admit that I thought the ACA was a half measure and unnecessary giveaway to the insurance companies and that the Libya invasion was a half planned out moral disaster but I might take them all over again before seeing either Mr. Trump or Secretary Clinton inhabiting the White House. So, I'm asking, is there any way for you to stay in office?

No matter who wins, what would happen if you just didn't leave and we the voters just sort of acted like this election had never occurred? We could just hold another election next year. We could still call it the 2016 Presidential Election even though it would be 2017. It could be a lie we all just play along with like trickle down economics or money not being an influence on policy.

Would Michelle be willing to do that? I know she's ready to leave. I mean, she's *ready* to get out of there. We can all tell and it makes total sense. She's sick of the limelight and the insults and even the constant repetitions from Democrats about how graceful she is probably don't make up for that. I work on the Internet. I get that. But still, maybe she would be willing to suck it up a little while longer for the good of the country? Maybe Biden could do all the heavy lifting while you two just live in Chicago? I dunno, I'm spitballing here.

Maybe that's selfish but c'mon, what are we supposed to do here? Either Trump gets elected and, if he gets his way, bankrupts the country with tax cuts and ushers in a leather clad era of dystopian street battles or Clinton gets elected and engages Russia in aerial combat over Syria while personally transferring every remaining blue collar job to Vietnam. There are no good options, Mr. President!

So, I'm asking you, as a favor to me, a person you do not know, just stick it out. When the election results come in we'll agree to ignore them and just pretend that the election is next year. Then maybe we can have the Presidential season we were supposed to get in the first place between John Kasich and Bernie Sanders. I'm pretty sure neither of those guys groped, assaulted, and insulted their way to success or gave a bunch of private speeches to Wall Street fat cats in order to make money and secure their support even after they wrecked the economy.

So, what do you say? Are you in? I'll pretend if you will.

29

Fuck You, Trump – My Baby Was 'Ripped Out Of My Womb' Because I Was Going To Die

Cecily Kellogg

I've written this story more times than I can count because people keep saying bullshit like what Trump said in the debate the other night. In case you were smart and didn't watch, here's what he said.

If you go with what Hillary is saying, in the ninth month, you can take the baby and rip the baby out of the womb of the mother just prior to the birth of the baby.

Now, you can say that that's OK and Hillary can say that that's OK. But it's not OK with me, because based on what she's saying, and based on where she's going, and where she's been, you can take the baby and rip the baby out of the womb in the ninth month on the final day. And that's not acceptable.

Listen, you fucking idiot. What you described literally never happens.

If a baby is near full term and the mother is sick — say, like me, dying from a pregnancy-related disease like preeclampsia—they deliver the fucking baby alive if possible. In fact, if the baby is past viability, they will whisk it to the NICU once born and do their damnedest to save that baby's life.

But here's the thing: viability varies. Fetuses, you might be surprised to know, grow at different rates and are impacted by different things so "viability" is fluid and is not a one-size-fits-all determination of the likelihood of the baby surviving outside the womb. And sometimes babies are so sick they won't survive—even in the ninth month of pregnancy. **Even so, those babies are DELIVERED, not "ripped out," you fucking asshole.**

Not that you'll listen to me, you selfish opportunistic prick, because I'm extremely low on your personal pussy grabbing scale being both old AND fat, but here's my story, briefly.

I fought like hell to get pregnant.

After our first IVF cycle, I was pregnant with twin boys. At a routine ultrasound appointment at 23 and a half weeks pregnant, we found out one of the twins had died. My doctor asked me to come from the ultrasound clinic to his office to chat once we learned this, and it was during that appointment that I was given three standard tests: I was weighed, my blood pressure was taken, and my urine tested for protein.

The results were terrible. My blood pressure was ridiculously high, I'd gained eighteen pounds of fluid in just a week or so, and my urine dipstick actually turned black because there was so much protein being shed by my body.

It was preeclampsia, a disease that effects some 5–8% of pregnancies. 76,000 women each year DIE from this disease. And guess what cures preeclampsia? Only one thing: ending the pregnancy.

Here's the good news: in most cases, preeclampsia develops later in pregnancy, and most of those babies are saved. This is fantastic, although it's also worth noting that preeclampsia is one of the leading causes of cerebral palsy.

But that's not what happened to me.

Once I was admitted to the hospital, I started getting sicker. I started vomiting. My blood pressure soared. My head hurt so badly I thought it would kill me. I stopped producing urine as my organs began to shut down. I was moments away from seizures, comas, and death — yes, motherfucker, DEATH—**when a team of doctors surrounded my bed and** told me I had to terminate the pregnancy or my surviving son and I would BOTH die.

Let me make this very, very clear: **this was the worst fucking day of my life.** It was absolutely wrenching, devastating, and horrid. My husband and I sobbed after we received the news.

We wanted those babies more than anything.

(Another note: if you tell me that the doctors lied to me and my surviving twin was far enough along to go to the NICU, go back and read what I said about viability. Because of the nature of my disease, my surviving twin was tiny and near death. He would not have lived. So spare me your "pro-life" bullshit links and faux kindness, m'kay?)

And my doctor—who happened to be only one of TWO doctors in the Philadelphia area who knew how do the procedure that would save my life—**said it was also the worst day of his professional career.** It sucked. For all of us. So fucking much.

Donald, what you described last night literally never happens. EVER. Nope, not once. Not ever. In EVERY SINGLE CASE of pregnancy termination done in the final trimester of pregnancy, it is because the mom is dying or the baby's condition is incompatible with life.

Do you understand? Oh, why the fuck did I even ask that. **Of course you don't.** Because you live in an alternate universe while the rest of us are over here living in motherfucking reality.

Asshole. Fuck you, Trump. Just that. FUCK YOU.

30

I'm Proud To Be A Nasty Woman

Ari Eastman

So, it's well known by now that at the third presidential debate, Trump referred to Hillary Clinton as *'a nasty woman.'*

People who closely follow me already know my political beliefs and honestly, that's not even what this is about. This election feels like mono—I'm too fucking tired for anything. We're all talking in circles, creating even larger divides and I just want to hibernate. It feels like every adult in the room is screaming and I'm a five-year-old kid who thought this party was gonna be fun.

I'm not interested in a huge political debate right now. And yet somehow, someone will inevitably comment that I'm wrong or spew some propagandistic shit that I'm not interested in reading right now.

What I do want to say is to all women who have felt triggered during this election cycle, you're not alone. And maybe what we need is something cheesy right now, like an affirmation. Is that dumb? Probably.

But whatever, here goes.

I'm a nasty woman. And maybe you're a nasty woman. Maybe being nasty means you're complex, multifaceted, never the kind of human you can stick in a box.

Here's to all the nasty women everywhere.

May you keep on being nasty. Because according to what I've seen, I think I've figured out what nasty *really* means. It means brilliant. It means accomplished. It means never backing down.

Maybe being nasty means you're confident, independent, loud, soft, tough, sensitive—anything and everything.

It means you're flawed. And a fighter. And damn, is there anything more admirable than that?

31

My Hometown And The Rise Of Donald J. Trump

Jacob Geers

A long cornfield separates the only two cities I have lived in my entire life.

The first, a sleepy suburb of Cincinnati. It is sprawling township nestled between an IKEA and popular amusement park *Kings Island*. Originally a farming community built around a gas station and Long John Silvers on the corner of Ohio interstate I-75, the town is now primarily populated with America's upper middle class. The parents of my childhood friends were engineers, lawyers, doctors, mid-level corporate executives, and small business owners. Few new home constructions sell for under $300,000.

In my formative years, I had the impression that my family and I lived in a fairly large house. We had not only a living room but also a "family room" in the basement. We had not two bathrooms, but three. We had a garage that my dad always planned to convert to an extra bedroom. We had a large window overlooking our large yard.

But as I grew older, a new world began rising around me. The expansive Dudley Farm which had for so long stretched the length of Tylersville Road was bulldozed for a shopping center. A stretch of street surrounded by ancient, lofty trees that we fondly referred to as the "tree tunnel" was sequestered in favor of a new subdivision. Property values skyrocketed as families moved in to take advantage of our exceptional school district (and then subsequently failed to vote for tax increases that would keep said district afloat). What it meant to be "middle class" was rapidly changing, and not in a good way.

My mom has spent her entire life here—she lives in the same neighborhood she was born into—and each year the place becomes more foreign to what she remembers. The new neighborhoods that rise out of the dirt these days have fancy names like "The Blah Estates" or "The Acres at Whatever" or "Wetherington." Our neighborhood doesn't have a name, and it's specifically neighborhoods like mine where the message of Donald Trump has caught fire.

When I talk to the parents of my friends who grew up in the fancy subdivisions with fancy names, they voted for John Kasich in the Ohio Primary and they balk at the notion of a President Donald J. Trump. Many of them are actually breaking a Republican voting streak and casting their lot with Hillary Clinton. Others are voting third party or writing in a name they find more suitable. And a few, of course, are holding their noses and voting for the Republican nominee—but not happily.

When you drive through the streets near my old house, you feel a radically different energy. "Trump / Pence" signs dot every other house. Giant homemade posters proclaiming, "Lock Her Up!!!" proudly stand nailed into the ground. Many boast unflattering pictures of Hillary Clinton behind bars. The passion for Trump's message on these streets is insatiable because the feeling of betrayal is universal.

Because—at the core of it—the message of Donald Trump is that someone has stolen something from you, and he'll get it back.

During the 2008 economic collapse, my neighborhood was dotted with an endless display of foreclosure signs that match the "Trump / Pence" signs seen today. The pain of recession was felt by nearly *everybody*, but the relief of recovery was felt by only a few. The people without college degrees who lost their jobs *never* found good ones to replace it. My dad is one of many who now works far too hard for far too little money. It wasn't the deal that the American dream promised them.

And, just a few miles away, in gated communities in the same township, many people have come out ahead. People who had college degrees, who had never laid brick or hauled freight in a warehouse. People who are perhaps perceived to have learned the rules of life in a classroom rather than in the "real world." People who often put a priority on social issues (*"who cares if men are allowed to make out with each other or not, I need a job!"*) rather than the pains of the working man. For them, the crude comments of Donald Trump are undesirable and crass but simply don't hold a candle to the greatest swindle in our history: that there are families who live within a square mile of each other who got vastly inequitable outcomes to their American dream.

And to people for whom civil rights and basic American liberties are not under attack or siege, there might not be a clear reason to not back Donald Trump. If you are white, male, heterosexual, cisgender, there is no obvious risk to backing a man who promises to retrieve the past and give it back to you in the present. Maybe they should know better, but maybe it's hard to know better.

───────────

The second town is the seat of Ohio's governance—the city of Columbus. I attended The Ohio State University for four years, and after graduation now still live in the city—sandwiched between my old college campus and the downtown area.

Columbus cringes at the notion of a Trump Presidency. Down every street there are Clinton / Kaine signs sticking out of tiny urban yards. For many here, the election is about values—and whether you have them or not. For a city that has been characterized as the gay Mecca of the midwest, boasts not only a diverse population—but one of the refugees—this election isn't about the issues. While perhaps some of the Franklin suburbs will show up for Trump, on November 8th country as a whole will be colored bright ruby blue for the former Secretary of State.

It is easy to go an entire day here without encountering any supporters of Donald Trump. Sure, there are certainly some working class whites and boozed up frat boys who will cast their vote for the TV businessman, but they are hard to find. And so it becomes easy to characterize anybody who supports Trump as clueless, "uneducated," or even evil. Maybe it's too easy.

"Racist," "Sexist," "Homophobic," "Transphobic," among others, are words used daily to summarize Donald Trump's supporters. But maybe we need to move beyond summary? Maybe casual summary and dismissal of "deplorables" are what cause them to become deplorable in the first place?

The left preaches tolerance, but it does not necessarily preach compassion.

As the polls have tightened over the past week, I have slowly been trying to get my mind prepared for the idea of Donald Trump ascending to the office of Washington, Roosevelt, and Lincoln. I've begun bracing myself for the gloating Twitter pepe trolls, the normalization of bigotry, and my right to marry get thrust back into public contention.

But I've also begun to consider the idea that perhaps the rise of Trump is not a result of our country being evil. Rather, it's a result of having two radically different Americas in one whole.

One neighborhood is filled with people who attained a college degree, is more insulated from economic turbulence, benefits from globalization, and too often sees itself as intellectually superior. Then another neighborhood, filled with people who have worked just as hard, for just as long (or perhaps longer) but has seen their economic security melt below their feet.

And then some half-rate billionaire tells them that they've been had, *and* there are specific people they can blame. He tells them that the world is unraveling, and they believe him, because *their* world is unraveling—and nobody else seems to care.

You Might Think That Hispanic And African Americans Can't Respect Trump Voters But The Truth Is The Exact Opposite

Daniel Hayes

On November 1st, highly-respected organization the Pew Research Center released a poll on how Trump voters and Clinton voters see one another. The poll broke things down by demographic response as well, as Pew polls often do. Given the common invective of this campaign season, you would be forgiven for believing that Hispanic Clinton supporters might have a lot of anger towards those Americans currently supporting Trump. However, you'd be wrong.

But first, let's look at the larger picture. Pew conducted this poll between October 20th and 25th, not long after the Access

Hollywood hot mic recording of Donald Trump engaging in "locker room talk", as Trump later described it, with Billy Bush. Additionally, the poll was conducted after Trump had been repeatedly accused of sexual assault.

Clinton supporting poll takers were asked to respond in one of two ways, either that they "have no trouble respecting someone who supports Donald Trump for President" or that they "have a hard time respecting someone who supports Donald Trump for President. The question was also asked of Trump supporters in the same way regarding Clinton supporters. Here are the overall results.

The results are interesting and, perhaps, somewhat counter-intuitive given the atmosphere at some Trump rallies and the decades-long opposition on the part of older Trump supporters to Hillary Clinton. More than half of Trump supporters polled, 56% have "no trouble" supporting Clinton supporters. On the other side, however, nearly 58% of Clinton supporters have a hard time respecting Trump supporters.

But once you dig into the demographics of these responses things get even more interesting.

Nearly six-in-ten Clinton supporters have a hard time respecting Trump voters

% of registered voters who say ...

Among Clinton supporters

| I have a **hard time** respecting someone who supports Donald Trump for president | I have **no trouble** respecting someone who supports Donald Trump for president |

| 58 | 40 |

Among Trump supporters

| I have a **hard time** respecting someone who supports Hillary Clinton for president | I have **no trouble** respecting someone who supports Hillary Clinton for president |

| 40 | 56 |

Notes: Based on registered voters who support each candidate.
Don't know responses not shown.
Source: Survey conducted Oct. 20-25, 2016.

PEW RESEARCH CENTER

via Pew Research

White women who back Clinton, in particular, say it's hard to respect Trump supporters

% of Clinton supporters who _____ respecting someone who supports Trump for president

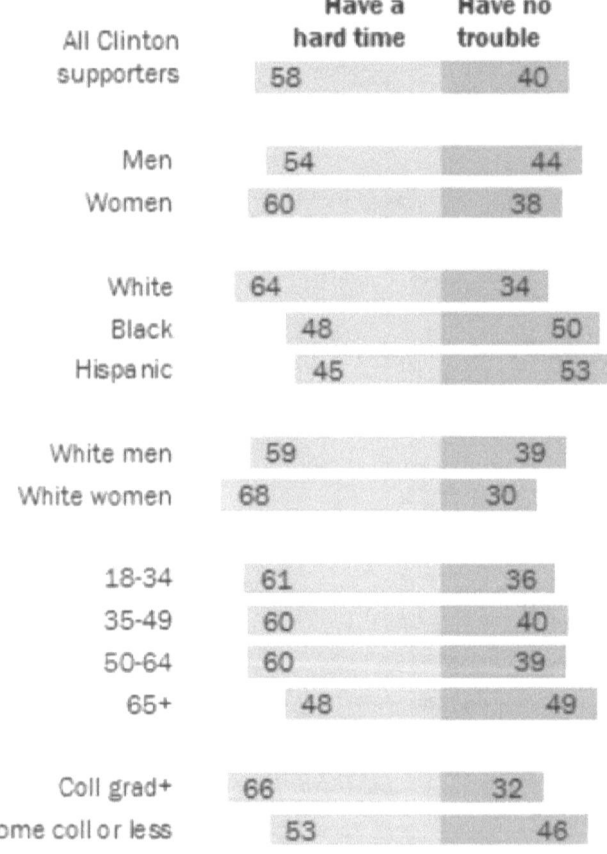

	Have a hard time	Have no trouble
All Clinton supporters	58	40
Men	54	44
Women	60	38
White	64	34
Black	48	50
Hispanic	45	53
White men	59	39
White women	68	30
18-34	61	36
35-49	60	40
50-64	60	39
65+	48	49
Coll grad+	66	32
Some coll or less	53	46

Notes: Based on registered voters. Whites and blacks include only those who are not Hispanic; Hispanics are of any race. Don't know responses not shown.
Source: Survey conducted Oct. 20-25, 2016.

PEW RESEARCH CENTER

Out of all the demographics polled, it is White women who

support Clinton that have the hardest time respecting someone who votes for Donald Trump and it's nearly uniform until you look at White women over the age of 65.

It's also exacerbated greatly by education level. White women who are college graduates have the hardest time respecting Donald Trump supporters of any demographic in the country.

Given Trump's early controversial statements about illegal immigrants that seemed to many to be conveying xenophobia towards Hispanics in general, one might think that Hispanics would have the most difficulty respecting Trump voters.

Additionally, given the opposition to Trump's campaign by African-American groups such as Black Lives Matter as evidenced at Trump's Chicago rally in March and the support for Trump among some White Nationalists, one might think that African Americans would also have a lot of difficulty respecting Trump voters.

However, these two groups of Clinton voters, Hispanics and African-Americans, are the *most* likely demographic to have *no trouble* respecting Trump supporters.

33

Why Did Ted Nugent Grope Himself On Stage While Campaigning For Donald Trump?

Jacob Geers

It seems to be a rite-of-passage for surrogates of Donald J. Trump to eventually lose their marbles. Rudy Giuliani totally forgot the 9/11 terrorist attacks happened at one point, alleged that Hillary Clinton was never at ground zero with him. Michael Cohen hilariously asked what polls showed Trump down, at a point of the campaign where all of them did. And now Ted Nugent—and already controversial figure—decided to grab his junk in front of a crowd assembled in support of Trump.

"I got your blue state right here, baby! Black and blue!" he yelled, grabbing the bulge in his pants.[1]

1. https://www.youtube.com/watch?v=GcEN6pHW53g

The crowd cheered wildly, but does anybody know what he means? Does he get blue-balled a lot by women once they hear him talk? Does he have a medical problem that needs to be addressed by a doctor? Is it a cry for help? Maybe Ted should go to Healthcare.gov, get some health insurance, and figure this problem out in a more private manner?

Thank Jesus this election is almost over.

34

Meet Evan McMullin, The Third Party Candidate Who Might Just Win Utah And Stop Donald Trump

Daniel Hayes

A product of the "Stop Trump" movement, Evan McMullin isn't a name that's heard as often in this Presidential season as Donald Trump's or Hillary Clinton's and that's because the eleven year CIA Operations Officer, former chief policy director for the House Republican Conference, and Wharton School of Business grad has only been in the race since early August.

Since then he's managed to get himself on the ballot in eleven states and will likely be available as a write-in in thirty-two others as an Independent. McMullin is running on a platform of fiscal responsibility and social and ethnic inclusivity that contradicts much of the rhetoric some members of the GOP have been engaged in for years now. A Mormon, McMullin has become especially popular in the state of Utah where he's polling four points ahead of Hillary Clinton and only five points behind Donald Trump.

I first met Evan McMullin in 2008 in Baghdad's International Zone (Green Zone). At the time he was an Operations Officer (Case Officer) doing counterintelligence and foreign intelligence work for the CIA. This was during the Spring and Summer and I was there for a few months backfilling for the full-time field Staff Operations Officers and Targeting Officers who were either rotating out or going on a much needed vacation.

The warmest months of 2008 in Baghdad were no cake walk even if you were in the IZ (International Zone). This was during the Jaysh al-Mahdi offensive and most nights you went to bed only after being sung a lullaby by the C-RAM (Counter Rocket and Mortar) klaxon. You woke up the same way, often in the middle of the night or before dawn, and ran to the bunker nearest your trailer. Yes, we slept in trailers. I slept in one with four bunks in it and Evan had one with a single bed, a perk of being stationed in Baghdad for an entire tour.

I lived this reality for a few months but he lived it for at least an entire year. We were both in our early 30s then and Evan was one of the older officers, most were in their 20s. He was also one of the bravest. Without speaking too much about methods, Evan was one of the few officers who would wander outside the IZ to meet with people who had information that the United States government needed to know. He would gear up along with others and head out to do his work.

Evan was brave but he didn't talk about it and he certainly

never crowed about it. He just did it. As a result of that hard work he was able to uncover photographic evidence of mass murder in Syria that no one else had been able to get despite swirling rumors that the Assad regime was engaging in such activities.

Evan was a good guy to work with and a fantastic team player who worked well with subordinates (like me). As anyone who's ever had a boss knows, that can be everything. He also knew how to take the lead and commanded the respect of senior officers who thought of him as competent and intelligent. I worked with him every day I was in Baghdad and our desks were back to back. We spoke on and off all day and, during stressful days when we were all scrambling, Evan kept a cool head.

There are many things about Evan's platform that I disagree with. As the descendent of share croppers and oil workers I have always been a dyed in the wool labor Democrat. I am socially liberal. Evan is a conservative and yet he isn't the kind of conservative that we have seen in a very long time. He has none of the mean-spiritedness present in this election nor the empty blustering of the current GOP nominee.

Evan cares about people who are different from him which is both a mark of a good person and a mature one. He knows more about the business of counterterrorism and the on-the-ground realpolitik of international relations than anyone else in today's Presidential race and, in my direct experience, he is honest. In our current contest between two highly unpopular candidates, one could do worse than vote for the brave, hard-working man from Utah who loves his country and wants to make it better, even if your beliefs don't line up with his all the way.

The Calamity Of America's Scientific Future Under A President Trump

Jayde Lovell

The 2016 Election is now on our doorstep, and most Americans have their own fears (and hopes… but mainly fears) about what the next 24 hours will bring. For a lot of 'science people' like myself, our particular fear is rooted in the potential disaster a Trump Presidency could bring on scientific research and innovation—and the resulting impact this would have on the US economy.

If Trump is elected (God forbid)—the evidence does not look good. Trump is a man who has described Global Warming as a hoax. He's said vaccines cause autism. He has pledged to withdraw from the Paris climate agreement, and reverse Obama's regulations for climate protection. Trump's running mate,

Mike Pence, is strongly against stem cell research, and could threaten to turn back the progress we've made in saving lives. Trump is a guy who goes around defaming our National Institute of Health.

We have every reason to believe that science could be the first in Trump's firing line if he becomes President. We all know that he does not like evidence, logic, facts and such.

It's so easy for politicians, especially one like Trump, to cut funding for science. We as a public don't often think about how much scientific progress that we've made. We don't walk around going 'Hey, guess what—I don't have polio right now!' Science just did it. We don't walk around going, 'Hey—guess what—I'm not dying of starvation!' We don't think about all the research that's gone into agriculture science. We don't walk around going 'It's so awesome that we're not dying from floods or typhoid in our dirty drinking water'. These things didn't just happen—they're the result of decades of scientific research and development.

That's why we created this video: 'What Has Science Ever Done For Us?[1]' to show just how much value science adds to our everyday lives. The video is a parody of *What Have The Romans Ever Done For Us?* a famous scene from *Monty Python's Life of Brian*. It depicts a bleak future where President Trump has applied austerity measures to science and innovation funding.

We thought the Monty Python scene was so relevant to the position we find ourself in today. Because, if you ask the ques-

1. https://www.youtube.com/watch?v=thqKO--xUok

tion 'What has science ever done for us?'—the answer is actually 'Everything'.

The reason that the US is a leader when it comes to innovation and technology is because they have extremely strong universities and research institutions, who've managed to attract the world's best talent into their public and private corporations. There's definitely a lot of backward steps that are easy to make and forward momentum that could be killed overnight.

It's a really scary position to be in, where, in a few months, scientists across the nation could find their funding cut. So voters really need to think about all the progress we've made and how much we have to lose.

I know who I'll be voting for—and it's not Trump. Or a third party.

36

Donald J. Trump Has Won The 2016 Presidential Election In A Stunning Come From Behind Victory

Daniel Hayes

New York City real estate businessman and former reality television host Donald J. Trump has won the 2016 Presidential election over former Secretary of State Hillary Clinton. Hillary Clinton has phoned Donald Trump to congratulate him on his victory.

The result was unexpected by many pundits and pollsters as Trump faced repeated accusations of past sexual harassment and assault after an audio recording emerged of Trump engaged in what he later called "locker room talk" with television host Billy Bush. Trump's popularity suffered uniformly in the polls immediately after the recording was released.

However, Clinton too faced an October surprise of her own when FBI Director James Comey announced that the bureau would be looking into additional emails pertaining to Clinton which came to light as the result of an investigation into disgraced former Congressman Anthony Weiner, the ex-husband of Clinton campaign Vice Chairwoman, Huma Abedin.

2016's Presidential election has been among the most contentious in recent history with an electorate and country seemingly more divided than it has been in decades. Soon-to-be President Trump who has promised to lower income tax rates to 15%, re-negotiate or nullify trade agreements and terms with nations such as Mexico and China, as well as building a wall of some kind along the Mexican border will face an uphill battle in implementing his legislative agenda.

Perhaps owing to these agenda items, President-elect Trump managed to pick off the blue collar states of Wisconsin and Michigan.

President-elect Trump will be sworn in on January 20th, 2017.

PART 5

On November 8th, 2016 the United States elected Donald Trump to be their next President.

By the afternoon the next day, we were inundated with responses to the election. While our audience tends to be more liberal, we received articles on all sides of the issue. We published as many as we could, giving people a voice on an election that was now wholly out of their control.

People expressed their fears at what the next four years would hold.

People expressed their anger at a country that could elect this man.

People expressed their frustration at the "other side."

People tried to understand, people tried to explain.

And we published it all.

37

Dear America, This Is My Prayer For You

Marisa Donnelly

I like to write about love. It feels relevant, feels important. It's a big part of my life, and the lives of those around me, and when I write about love, I feel the layers of my heart reopening and healing and connecting with strangers. And that's so beautiful.

But today, I don't feel like I can write about love. Not about love and relationships, broken hearts and missing people you've drifted from. Today those things seem trivial. Today there are more pressing issues and heartaches.

Today we have become a divided nation.
Today we have become a fearful nation.

Today so much has changed and when I woke up this morning, all I could see was status after status about the future of this nation. And it hurts me.

It hurts that there are people fearing for their lives. It hurts that there are souls who are scared, who are doubting their next move, who are nervous and unsure and angry. It hurts that even in the wake of this important decision, America is in a state of unrest.

I don't know if I can put into words my own feelings, let alone my reaction to what I've seen, to what I've read, to the bleeding hearts I've encountered, so desperately divided.

But what I do know, is that I can write about love. Love for our new president, love for our country, love for one another despite our differences. Because love and prayer are really the only two things we have.

Today marks a new day of a new path, and whether or not we support it, we can support America with love.

Whether or not we agree with Donald Trump as our president, we can choose to pray for our nation. To trust that these changes are in God's hands, and ask him to lead our country to a place of strength, acceptance, tolerance, equality and respect.

This is not a political piece, not an 'I support(ed) this candidate,' or a 'here's my perspective on the election.' This is simply a statement of support for America, for each other, for love in the wake of this election.

What we wanted, who we voted for, which candidate had our support is

irrelevant now. What matters is how we move forward, how we love, how we show compassion, and who we become.

And so I pray for our healing. I pray for those who are frightened, that they would know that God is with them, even on their darkest days. I pray for those who feel disrespected, that they would see their power, their beauty, their worth in the eyes of our Father. I pray for me, for you, for our neighbors and enemies and friends—that despite our perspectives, we can find acceptance.

I pray for love because love is what we do next. We love. And we continue to love.

I am a woman. And yes, I have been challenged by the perspectives of this new leader of our country. Yes, I have been hurt by the way he has treated my sex, by the things he has said about people that I love and know and don't know. Yes, I have been angered by the decisions he has made.

But this isn't about me. And this isn't about the past.

The truth is, we can only look forward, not back. And we must continue forward by putting our fears in the arms of Christ. We must ask Him to heal our hearts, to forgive the sins we've made and encountered, and ask Him to guide the future of this nation.

We must ask Him to guide our president, to love our president, to be with our president in all the words he says and decisions he makes.

We must not keep ourselves at arm's length from one another, spewing hateful words and living in darkness. We must not hold onto our perspectives, so much so, that it keeps us from coming together. We must not let our fears hold us back from becoming a powerful nation.

Whether or not we agree with the decision we have made, we must learn to forgive one another and trust in God. We must pray for our president, our nation, our future, and our broken neighbors. We must find a way to come together, for that is the only way our America will survive.

We must love. And keep loving.

38

To Everyone Currently Saying 'Donald Trump Is #NotMyPresident'

Lane Farrell

Trump's victory has shown the underbelly of American politics true colors. I have seen terrible reactions from fellow conservatives, and I have seen equally as horrible reactions from liberals. Perhaps one of the most concerning has been Democrats claiming that Donald Trump is not my President.

I have two words for you:

He is.

Public opinion showed that nobody liked either candidate. Words like anger, fear, repression, racist, and liar have been thrown around to the point that we are all desensitized. Let's take a second to stop and think about the real implications of this election and exactly why Donald Trump is, in fact, your President.

First of all, we choose to abide by the democratic system in America by maintaining our citizenship here. Part of that great privilege is to honor the system. Hillary Clinton herself conceded to obey the system and recognized that we need to support Donald in his endeavors as President; I find it baffling that her supporters are swearing her last sentiment off. If you are truly in disarray about Clinton's loss, find yourself a job in politics and start working towards the next election.

Obama was the President for the last eight years, but the Republicans did not just take back the White House. We took back the House and Senate, most seats by popular and electoral vote. This speaks to a broader public dissatisfaction. **The Presidency is bigger than any one person; soldiers serving our country die for the President. People serving our country will die for Trump. We need to honor the institution.**

Most importantly I want you to know this. The average American makes $24,000 a year and lives in suburban to rural areas. Almost my entire social network complaining about Clinton's loss went to The George Washington University, a school that prides itself on political awareness or lives near me in the Financial District of Manhattan. Most of you paid three times what the average American makes to attend college or your work in banking in one of the most expensive neighborhoods in New York.

You are privileged; you are not representative of the broader country.

I am truly sorry for your loss, but Donald Trump is your President just as Obama was mine.

39

Why Foreigners Are Heartbroken Over The U.S. Presidential Election

Sade Andria Zabala

Today I woke up and it feels like the entire world is burning.

When you have clinically diagnosed anxiety, it can often feel like everything around you is on fire. Sometimes for no reason I get palpitations when I'm standing in a public area full of strangers, other times I feel sick while sitting in the car next to my husband because my brain and body tell me they can feel the Earth moving on its axis. Bile rises to my throat as I get dizzy and claustrophobic.

Most days I can calm myself down. If it gets real bad I get my 'happy pills' and wait for them to kick in. But often I don't need to resort to that, I am usually able to silently repeatedly tell myself "It's okay, this isn't real, it'll be over soon" and after half-an-hour or so the feeling of panic dissipates to something more controllable.

But not today.

No amount of meds, or meditation, or positive thinking is making my head stop spinning or helping me make sense of reality.

Not today after waking up to Donald Trump getting elected. Not today after heartbreakingly finding out some of my loved ones misguidedly support him. Not today after Brexit, after the continuing terrorist attacks all over the world, after David Bowie's death and Alan Rickman's, after ISIS, after daily police brutality. Not today after the Philippine supreme court ruled that a dictator is allowed to be buried in the "Cemetery For Heroes" because hey, the current President says it's okay. Not today when many poor are dying in my country under the guise of patriotism and my people support it. Not today when my country bleeds for the sins of a shitty-person-become-president and my people tell us to "get over it, move on." Not today when the USA seems to be doing the same—ignoring lessons from history by electing a sexist, hateful, racist, inexperienced, ill-tempered, unstable, incompetent white man.

I've casually voiced my opinion on social media in a (I feel) polite manner. I didn't call anyone a Repulicunt or a libtard or any other slur. I've attempted to articulate my disappointment and hurt towards people I personally know who support this Cheeto AKA poor excuse of a person.

Not only I but many others who also expressed their thoughts and feelings even more gracefully were met with a resounding—"You don't even live here! You don't know anything! The US is none of your business!"

How poignant yet ignorant.

The US is arguably the most powerful and influential country in the world. The fact that nearly everybody holds their breath every US Presidential Election is testament of that. And the resounding cry of shock after today's result is even more concrete proof.

Your politics affects my country's. It affects India's, Pakistan's, Belgium's, France's, etc. Not only are right-wing politicians in Europe (and probably North Korea, China, and Russia) rejoicing over this massive political shift, the US Presidential Election results determines the future of many countries' economies.

For instance, Donald Trump The Cheeto thinks that climate change isn't real and is something that the Chinese invented. Um, okay. That said, along with his campaign to cease outsourcing from different countries, there's probably going to be a dip in the manufacture, usage, and practice of alternative energy. Denmark recently made a deal with the US to equip the latter with wind turbines. With Trump's cray-cray threats and "platforms," Danes predict an unfortunate low for the wind industry which will further knock down their already shaky economy.

For the life of me, I can't imagine why any intelligent, respectful person would exclaim to civil foreigners to "shut up" about US politics because we "know nothing." Maybe we're not political analysts, maybe we don't have American citizenship, maybe we were not born there or live there—but this affects all of us. Your misguidedness (which could've been projected into something more positive but e-mails are scarier than a narcissistic racist sexual abuser) affects all of us. Donald Trump's hate campaign affects all of us.

BESIDES—I'm confident many of us foreigners actually READ UP AND RESEARCHED extensively about your own candidates and political-economical news way before the preliminaries even began. I'm not as confident in saying the same about most of Trump supporters, though, but I may be in the wrong. Still, we have at least the knowledge to be able to voice an educated and informed opinion.

Frankly, we are in fear for our friends and loved ones. Those who ARE American close to our hearts who happen to be homosexual, transexual, female, Latino, Black, Middle-Eastern, Muslim—all our loved ones who are not CIS and white. I've literally gotten calls and text messages from four of my friends living in the US expressing their hopelessness. One of them, a female who is a survivor of sexual assault herself, was in tears. People that we've grown up with or met and built real camaraderie with are hurt and afraid. And to see them get attacked / instigated further on social media by Trump supporters after the devastating news that their society supports ignorance, hate, and the possible eradication of their rights and identity—this is not okay.

America, this is not okay.

Yes, you have the right to your vote. But I also have a right to think you fucked up big time and astoundingly proved the stereotypes that Americans are stupid. The rest of the world has the right to dislike Trump, be disappointed, and speak out about it. You have the right to your opinion (how poorly and crudely worded it may be), but as do I, as do we, as do the rest of the world (real freedom and democracy sucks, huh?).

Historically, the USA was an oppressor—a growing super-power which sought even more power by oppressing lesser countries such as my Philippines. America continues to bully the helpless states like that of Palestine and the world tries to forgive you for that anyway. We forgave you for these and so many other atrocities. We forgave you even when you never apologized because you actually seemed to evolve and grow from your mistakes. The results of this election, however, is a sign that you have willfully, purposely decided to regress—for hopelessness? for pride? for religion? for nationalism? for xenophobia?—and that we can not forgive.

"I wonder from where so many Americans get the idea that voting is supposed to be some expression of your deep-est, most beloved values and virtues rather than a prag-matic, political move meant to shift your country as much closer to your ideal as possible. This strikes me as another example of extreme individualism. Voting isn't about *you*. It's about your city, state, and/or country. It doesn't have to feel transcendently good deep down in your bones. It just has to *do* as much good as you can do, in this par-ticular moment in time."—brutereason

I'll continue to strive to treat you with respect despite so many of you laughing at "Libtards" and telling them to "accept" this ugly orange hypersexual mutant. I'll continue to respect your vote and your country's decision to elect a(nother) rich white dude who has shown he has zero respect for women and even less skill on how to run a country.

But I'll never respect the decision to support hate. To support ignorance AND hate whilst ironically calling ignorant those of us who bothered to make an effort to learn about your country's politics.

As my American friend, Tina Hatch, said, "[sic]Hateful comments (towards Hillary voters) only reinforce the low opinion people have of Trump and those who ardently follow him while they excuse his behaviors. **Don't tell people they have to unify behind this man. Show them why they should.**"

God bless the world.

40

Here's What Happened In The 2016 Election, And What *Needs* To Happen Next

Mitch King

How did we get here?

The President-elect of the United States of America has no previous political experience and is best known for parroting "You're fired" into millions of American households on a second-rate reality television program.

There's so much to unpack. There's so much to think about.

At the end of the day, what we've seen is a fundamental break down in the way American politics work. The media, the polls, and the candidates themselves—nothing worked.

The Media

The media worked in Trump's favor from the very day he announced his candidacy. The political circus was a show that none of America could turn away from, and Donald Trump was its star. At each step along the way, Trump's miscues were met with unprecedented publicity. Mock a reporter with a disability? The networks will run it for a week. Fire your campaign manager? No bother, CNN will pick him up right where you drop him off. Talk about grabbing any woman you want by the pussy? We'll skewer the other person in the video but won't even push you on the topic when given the chance. The hands of the media are implicit in this crime; not just as Trump's "dishonest media," but as biased, unethical, ratings-hungry idiots.

The Polls

What happened with the polls? Through about 3pm on Election day everything seemed fine. And then something flipped. Donald Trump was quickly gaining steam. He took Florida. He took North Carolina. He took Ohio. How was none of this predicted? Polls aren't ever going to be perfect. That's an impossible request. The most we can do is figure out why the polls were so off. One might also ask why we focus so much on the polls. They allowed us to become way more confident in victory than we probably should have been. I don't know many people that were anticipating it even being close, much less a loss. We've got to figure out how to forecast the outcomes of our elections, if only because we all want to avoid the gut-punch that came late Tuesday night.

The Candidates

Hillary Clinton and Donald Trump couldn't be more different in their campaign strategies. We can argue day and night about what each camp did right and wrong: Clinton should have gone to the rural parts of the country more, Trump's rhetoric really hurt him with inner cities, et cetera ad infinitum. What we do know is this: Clinton and Trump are both polarizing figures to huge chunks of the nation's populace. Whether its emails, or Benghazi, or simply being a woman in power, there are people that truly dislike Hillary Clinton. Likewise, Trump has his own dissenters for a ton of different reasons: xenophobia, sexual assault, and that damn leathery orange skin chief among them.

One candidate won, the other lost. That's how contests go. What I don't want us to forget is that one election does not make or break the country. There are people that feel emboldened to go out and show their bigotry to the nation, using Trump's election as validation. We can't let that happen, no matter what side of the line you fall on.

The "let's be united" rhetoric is tiring, especially in the wake of an election that so many people just wanted to be over. But we can't pretend not to see bigotry and hatred and call it out. We can't sit by and watch as our friends, our family, our neighbors, our coworkers are targeted and attacked. Call it out. Be a voice for those that don't have one. Amplify voices that need amplifying. Work with people and groups that fight for what you believe in. Change doesn't have to come from the top. The top can't stand without the supports at the base. Be that change at the bottom, and help send it through the entire system until the top has no choice but to change.

This is not the time to abandon America. This is when you hold on, hunker down, strap in, and fight for the America you want her to be. She's twisted out of shape, and her screws might be rusted, but she's weathered 240 years of crazy shit before. I think she can handle 4 more.

41

I Will Not Accept A 'Pussy Grabber' Administration

Sarah R. Hughes

What does being an American mean anymore? I used to think I know, but this election has made me reexamine a lot of what I thought I understood about this country, its people. Americans are from America, that part is obvious. However, if the election showed us anything, it's that they all clearly want different things.

It is ironic that the diversity of opinion, culture, race, and ethnicity that brought America together is now once again front and center, tearing it apart. It seems half the nation is accepting and tolerant, and the other half may be too, but they might be too accepting and tolerant. I get made fun of, often, for being a part of the "tolerant left" when I speak up about an injustice.

"You intolerant piece of shit," I have heard from Republicans, friends, family, and strangers alike.

But can you be too tolerant? Can we call it too tolerant to not only be okay with the KKK, a well-known hate group openly celebrating the election results? Can we call it too tolerant to openly celebrate with them? Is it tolerance or sexism that caused half of America to hear the sexual assault stories of several women and look the other way, voting for the accused?

Similarly, am I intolerant for my distaste for hate groups? I want them gone? I would like those people to leave. Yes, I am highly intolerant of racism, sexism, homophobia, bigotry, xenophobia, misogyny…sadly, so many things that were front and center throughout this election. Not only were they front and center, they were defended. We put the chance to lead the nation in the hands of a learning disabled, self-tan addict and defended his actions.

When he said he could grab women by the pussy, people defended him. *Women* defended him. Women demonized his accusers. When he made it clear he did not understand how the government worked, let alone had the vocabulary to speak to anybody who works in the government, we defended that too. As we learned he once called a pageant winner Miss Piggy due to her weight gain, some admitted she had put on weight, instead of pointing out perhaps that is what all people do, gain and lose weight. The weight was not the biggest issue. When he called her Miss Housekeeper based entirely on her race, nobody said a thing.

Well, not anybody. Some people spoke up. Many, in fact. And we were somehow demonized for being intolerant of a future leader, a great man, a man who was somehow being misunderstood despite his slew of accusations, trail of lawsuits, and failed attempts to run a successful business. We were at fault for pointing out his lack of common decency or concern toward *all* Americans, just the white and uneducated ones.

And even now as many of us continue to point out the various flaws, of which there are many, in his success, we are told to be quiet. We are asked to unify with those who accepted a ticket promoting conversion therapy for homosexuals. I was a ticket openly endorsed by the KKK. It was a ticket promising to cut off easy access to birth control and require mandatory funerals for miscarried and aborted babies despite the psychological damage it may due to the individual mother or woman.

I have had an abortion. I am not a mother. I did not want to bury the issue nor did I see the point. Had I had it my way, it would have been donated for stem cell research. This, I am sure, will not be an option for a very long time under a Pussy Grabber administration. And I am sure as I call him that I will be labeled intolerant once more. An extreme feminist, or a baby killer. Who knows what they will call me or us this time. I do not care. What I care about is the underlying and systemic hatred in the country that I was naively blind to until the former host of the fucking *Apprentice* won the presidential election.

A man who ran a fraudulent university stood before us all, saying the words "education" and "bigly," making it sound as though it would be better in the future if we let him control the nation. He had children with three wives, stating wildly inappropriate sexual things about his daughter while claiming to have solid Christian values. This is the person 50% of America looked to for leadership. He laughed smugly as Don King used the N word in a black church, while an African American woman grimaced nearby.

Yet I am the asshole for bringing these things up, for being ashamed that he has won, for admitting the last two years were not an election but a Jerry Springer show. And I still don't know why. What I do know is I am ready to turn to those who reject hate and violence with a hug and kindness in an effort to move forward, looking past this presidency to the light at the end of the tunnel.

42

An Open Letter To All The Moderate Right Wingers Who Voted For Trump

Kasey Altman

By now, you are sick of all the name-calling. For days, you've been accused of being a less than desirable person. You are tired of being categorized as racist, sexist, homophobic, misogynistic assholes.

When in reality, you're none of these things.

You believe women deserve equal opportunities. You believe opportunities become available to those that work hard enough. You believe hard work can translate to financial success, no matter where you came from.

You can't stand high taxes, maybe because you have someone

near and dear to your heart that worked their tail off to provide for you and your family.

You consider the people that take advantage of the welfare system and it makes your skin crawl. You believe it is unjust and unfair to provide financial stability for those people when they have done nothing to deserve it.

Like me, you've never been overtly racist. You have friends of all ethnicities and have never thought twice about their roots.

You've never considered it being irregular when a woman gets hired into corporate America. You agree that women can do just about anything a man can.

You and I share each and every one of these beliefs.

What makes us different?

Understand that the slander you are experiencing is not necessarily a reflection of your personal values. This is likely because your values do not align with this hatefulness.

Racist? Sexist? Homophobic? Misogynistic?!

Until now, when have you ever been any of these things?

Here is my explanation.

It is not about who you are and what your personal values might be. It is rather about who –and what– you have promoted in this election.

Your vote promotes racist, sexist, homophobic, misogynistic

innuendoes. Your vote enables the incitement of hate within this campaign to perpetuate. Your vote supports every Trump fan that has ever held a confederate flag, shouted racial slurs, and promoted gender inequality. Your vote supports homophobic remarks, and your vote supports unequal opportunities. Your vote supports infidelity. Your vote supports hypersexualisation of the female body. Your vote supports hypersexualisation of the male body. Your vote supports inappropriate remarks, insults, and hypocrisy.

Above all, your vote supports sheer hatred that has been incited within this campaign.

So, no: You have never considered yourself an overtly racist, sexist, misogynistic, homophobic asshole… Because you probably aren't.

But promoting a campaign like such makes you an enabler.

And you have enabled spite to speak.

Love trumps hate, always.

43

Dear Democrats: This Is Why Hillary REALLY Lost

James Swift

Hello, Hillary supporters.

Right now, I know you're still pretty dumbfounded and crest-fallen about that whole election deal. By now, you've wept a thousand tears and made a thousand angsty Twitter posts and maybe even protested the outcome of a 100 percent legitimate, democratically determined election by blocking public infra-structure and setting American flags on fire.[1]

But like it or not kids, you're going to have to emerge from your safe space cocoon and accept the cold, hard reality: yes, Donald Trump is going to be the next President of the United States, and Hillary Clinton, well, *isn't.*

---

1. https://www.thesun.co.uk/news/2147684/violence-erupts-across-the-us-as-pro-clinton-fans-riot-after-donald-trumps-shock-election-win/

Now, for a lot of you, this is the first time you've experienced something we like to call "losing." Yes, it's a fairly obscure word in today's "everybody gets a trophy" social milieu, but basically, it means instead of getting exactly what you want (or even believe you are *entitled* to), *you don't*. Instead, you have to *admit* that someone did better than you did in direct competition. A bizarre idea, I know, but hang with me here—as unsavory as it may sound, it's actually *beneficial for you*. In fact, as you folks are mighty keen on calling it, you could even describe it as "a learning experience."

You do know this has happened before, right? Oh yes, it certainly did. Let me take you back to a magical time called "the year 2004."

Back then, there was this big, mean, old grey-headed Republican man nobody liked.[2] Everybody called him a racist and a sexist and a homophobe and a bigot and an idiot and people all over the world protested whenever he so much as gave a speech about Medicare Part D reform (don't worry, that only affects old people—it's OK if you've never heard of it.) They said he was a sociopath and a baby killer and somebody who really, really hated Muslims and black people. They wanted him impeached for crimes against humanity. They literally burned effigies (that's like a pinata, except without the candy) in city streets and *prayed for his death*.

All of the Democrats and liberal sympathizers in Hollywood and the media, naturally, didn't like him one bit. So for an entire year, they made a coordinated effort to derail his campaign and get this other old grey-headed white dude elected.[3]

2. https://en.wikipedia.org/wiki/George_W._Bush

There were films at the local Cineplex that basically served as two-hour long attack ads.[4] Some of the most respected "journalists" in the history of the medium simply made up stories[5] about the guy they didn't like in the hopes that he would lose. MTV stars trotted out an entire campaign dedicated to mobilizing young voters to get out and vote because their "very identities were threatened"[6] by the mean old Republican boogeyman.

And the Democrats were convinced—100 percent convinced—that they had the election won a month ahead of time. I mean, after all of the money and airtime they sunk into getting the Democrat man elected, how could they possibly lose, especially to such a mean, old doo-doo head like the Republican candidate?

But then, something *terrible-awful* happened. When it came time for people to actually get out and vote, by golly, more people—*those horrendously misled people*—had the audacity to go out there and vote for the guy *that wasn't* supposed to win. The Democrats were agog; even after harnessing the full power and reach of big media to ridicule, mock, shame and label anyone who disagreed with them as white trash, racists and neo-Nazis, Middle America—you know, the 100 million or so Americans without college degrees who do stupid things for a living like deliver mail and put up drywall[7]—*refused to vote Democrat,*

3. https://en.wikipedia.org/wiki/John_Kerry
4. https://en.wikipedia.org/wiki/Fahrenheit_9/11
5. https://en.wikipedia.org/wiki/Killian_documents_controversy
6. http://whatzhotandnot.com/wp-content/uploads/2013/09/vote-or-die.jpg
7. http://www.forbes.com/sites/akelly/2015/04/28/the-neglected-majority-what-americans-without-a-college-degree-think-about-higher-education-part-1/%23616b60db6f0d

and somehow, that mean old Republican man *actually won the election.*

Hmm. Does that sound even remotely similar to something that may have happened a couple of days ago? Like, around November 8, perhaps?

History, as the old adage goes, is a fate destined to be repeated by those who forget it. And for the modern incarnation of the Democratic Party—the identity-politics and virtue signaling sorts they are—history as they *remember* it didn't begin until 2008. In that, the utter Democratic meltdown of 2016 is almost a *note-by-note* remake of the song and dance from 2004's election—the liberals got smug, they spent too much time attacking the *character* of their opponent instead of his actual economic and foreign policies and instead of *explaining* why their campaign platform would improve the lives of potential Republican voters, they instead sought to *shame them away* with a rich panoply of ill-defined, scientifically difficult to determine pejoratives like "racist" and "fascist."

And in *both* election cycles, the Democrats forgot that half the country existed. They forgot about the working class and lower middle class families in the Rust Belt, Appalachia and the rapidly deteriorating exurbs of Florida, North Carolina and Georgia—the kind of people whose biggest fear isn't being triggered by people wearing sombreros at football games[8], but having their job outsourced to India and going bankrupt because their health insurance premiums have literally *doubled* and *tripled* since the Affordable Care Act went into effect[9]. The

---

8. http://latino.foxnews.com/latino/lifestyle/2016/09/20/activist-cries-foul-after-west-point-fan-wears-sombrero-at-game-near-mexican/

Hillary campaign bet the farm that a leaked audio recording of Trump talking about groping women would give them the election. Alas, the sexual escapades of a billionaire real estate mogul don't mean a damn thing to the 52 percent of Americans who can't afford to spend more than $100 a month on health coverage.[10] Making a symbolic *pro-multiculturalism* stand does nothing for the 40 percent of Americans—yes, you heard me right, *40 percent*[11]—out of the workforce. Going on social justice warrior crusades to stamp out microaggressions is a downright insult to to the non-college educated laborers who have seen their pay decrease by nearly 10 percent over the last 20 years, while income for the college educated has increased by nearly *25 percent*[12]. While the Democratic Party ceaselessly criticized Trump supporters as racists and bigots and Islamophobes, they totally overlooked the single most appealing element of his platform to America's downtrodden, low-wage workers—namely, his plan to *eliminate any federal tax liability for those earning less than $25,000 a year.*[13]

There is a tremendous, tremendous lesson to be learned here. No political candidate, Republican or Democrat, can win an election based on identity politics instead of *socioeconomic politics*. You cannot virtue signal your way to the White House—if you run a campaign based *simply* on the fact you believe yourself to be *ethically superior* to the political other, as Hillary did, you **will** lose.

9. http://www.nytimes.com/2016/10/25/us/some-health-plan-costs-to-increase-by-an-average-of-25-percent-us-says.html?_r=0
10. http://www.nytimes.com/2016/10/25/us/some-health-plan-costs-to-increase-by-an-average-of-25-percent-us-says.html?_r=0
11. http://fortune.com/2015/09/14/donald-trump-unemployment-rate-jobs/
12. http://www.csmonitor.com/Business/2016/1006/Working-class-white-men-see-incomes-drop-How-is-that-changing-America
13. http://money.cnn.com/2015/09/28/news/economy/trump-income-taxes/

And if your election gameplan revolves around screaming about how "racist" and "misogynistic" and "homophobic" the counter-ideology is—rather than soundly explaining how *your* political platform *improves the lives* of the majority of Americans – *your campaign is already doomed.*

Donald Trump did not win—as many aggrieved liberals continue to claim—because America is a hotbed of white misogyny and racism (as evident by the fact that 42 percent of female voters[14] and nearly a *third* of the nation's Hispanic voters[15] cast their ballots for him *instead of her*). Trump won because his ads focused on economic growth and curtailing the slow creep of globalization (an absolute death sentence for what's left of American industry) while Clinton ran ads focused on how his comments *may make middle school girls feel insecure about their weight.*[16] Trump won because his political speeches revolved not around *how historic it would be if he was elected* but his blueprint to bring back the American School of Economics[17]. Trump won because instead of glossing over the ballooning costs of the ACA, he confronted them head on *and* detailed a seven-prong health care reform plan to lower costs *and* expand coverage[18].

But more than anything, dear Democratic friends, what cost Hillary the election … was you.

You attended ritzy colleges—almost certainly on the public

14. http://www.pewresearch.org/fact-tank/2016/11/09/behind-trumps-victory-divisions-by-race-gender-education/
15. http://www.usatoday.com/story/news/politics/elections/2016/2016/11/09/hispanic-vote-election-2016-donald-trump-hillary-clinton/93540772/
16. http://www.shape.com/lifestyle/mind-and-body/ad-hillary-clinton-campaign-body-image-presidential-race
17. https://en.wikipedia.org/wiki/American_School_(economics)
18. https://www.donaldjtrump.com/positions/healthcare-reform

dime—and grew up in well-to-do, upper-middle-class families (some of you, legitimate multi-millionaire[19] heirs) yet spent the entire campaign bemoaning *how* oppressed you were by the non-existent "privilege" of trailer park inhabitants and uninsured sheet metal workers. Your golden idols Bill Maher and Rachel Maddow and Van Jones never gave up an opportunity to belittle Trump loyalists as racists and idiots and unlearned white trash (ironically, while championing *themselves* as "the party of tolerance.") Instead of coming up with *counter-arguments* to Trump's policies on economic nationalism, you filled your Facebook and Twitter feeds with the same old boring refrain of "he's a big meanie and hurts our feelings, so he shouldn't be President."

And as fate would have it, failing to adequately explain how your economic and foreign policies benefit working class families in favor of just calling them "racists" and "misogynists" for not agreeing with you *isn't* the best way to win an election.

Try to keep that in mind for 2020, dear Democrats—unless, of course, you plan on losing *again*.

19. http://www.stltoday.com/lifestyles/columns/joe-holleman/mizzou-hunger-strike-figure-from-omaha-son-of-top-railroad/article_20630c03-2a68-5e63-9585-edde16fe05f3.html

44

I Just Said My Vows, But Now I'm Afraid President Trump Will Take My Marriage Away

Celeste Seymore

Amazed. Terrified. Nauseated. These were all the feelings that passed through my body as I frantically scrolled through my Twitter feed at 3 AM this morning. I had fallen asleep and hoped when I woke that I might wake up to the United States' first female President.

Instead, I woke in a nightmare.

I have been anxious about this election for the past two weeks. Perhaps I was an ignorant teenager before, but this was the first election where I realized that the issues at hand affected me directly. After all, I'm a gay woman, and on November 12th, 2016, I'm getting married.

Along with everyone else, I completed my civic duty and voted. I will always appreciate the act of voting. Because we were all there: black, white, gay, straight, trans and all other diversities. We were equal when we entered the booth and cast that ballot. **While we weren't voting for the same person, we were all able to vote. While we all had differing views, we were united in our right to express that opinion.**

I felt a similar swell of pride when my fiance and I applied for our Marriage License. While we were the only same-sex couple in the Charleston County Probate Court and received multiple glares from other couples, the clerk handed back our completed certificate and we left. We walked out as equals.

When I woke up this morning, I couldn't believe what I was reading.

A man who has groped women, mocked people, and openly attacked people who were different is going to be President. A man whose Vice President is a proponent of conversion therapy, the very thing that led to my depression at age 18, was elected to office. **I am not concerned. I am terrified.**

In a few days, I will sign my marriage certificate and legally become a spouse. In the back of my mind, I have had the bitter thought: How long before it's taken away? How many decades of work have we put in to see it disappear within the course of a few hours?

This is the man that America has chosen to lead. This election has torn friends, spouses, and families apart. And what should have unified us all last night drove an even bigger wedge between all of us. On one side, those convinced that this is the moment that has saved our country and the other side fearing that this is what will destroy it.

But we can't give up—we have to continue to fight for an America where all of us are equal, not just select groups.

Today we mourn, but tomorrow we work.

45

Dear Donald Trump: My Father, My Biracial Family, And Those Like Us, Are What Make America Great

Gabi Crowley

Dear Mr. Trump,

I think you have a lot to learn in this crazy little thing that we call life. No, definitely not from me. I'm just a 25-year-old female who probably fits somewhere in between your categories of "Miss Piggy" and "Miss Housekeeping."

The person that I think you can learn a thing or two from is my own father. My *White* father. A man who retired from the Detroit Public Schools system after teaching for more than 30 years. My father, who helped raise two daughters in the inner city of Detroit, while showing the utmost respect for them and his wife day in and day out. **A man who has emphasized equality for all, through his words and actions, always teaching me that I am not less nor greater than any other being.**

My father was raised in the city of Marquette, a predominantly White, small town, in the Upper Peninsula of Michigan, before deciding to travel the world in his twenties. After hitchhiking through Europe and perfecting his Spanish while living in Spain, he settled back down in the US and began his career as a special education teacher in the City of Detroit. Yes, that's correct. **A teacher for individuals, whom you, in fact, have publicly made fun of in the past simply because they are different than you.**

In his late 20's my father met my mother. A woman who is 100% Mexican, whose parents' first language is Spanish. A woman he would have never met if her grandmother didn't first enter this country illegally (Fun Fact: She later became a citizen after answering "Jorge Washington" when asked who the first President was in her citizenship interview). A few years later, my father married my mother, and in doing so, her large, loud family…or "hombres" as you so ignorantly refer to them as.

Instead of seeing my mother's relatives as "criminals," "rapists," and "killers," my father saw doctors, teachers, lawyers, mothers, fathers, and children.

I think it's safe to speak for my father and say that contrary to your past statements, **Mexico has indeed given us some**

of "the best." What I want you to know Mr. Trump, is that instead of building a wall (as you so vocally want to do if elected), and starting a life with someone that bared the same skin tone, beliefs, background, and past, my father created a bridge made out of love and respect. He fell in love with my mother, regardless of the color of her skin (Side note: really glad I have her genes…the man gets fire-engine red when he's out in the sun for more than 20 minutes). And regardless of her lack of blonde hair and blue eyes, or the fact that her family celebrates Christmas with tamales, rice, and beans instead of turkey, mashed potatoes, and gravy, my father saw and still sees my mother as a person, an individual, someone who is utterly and entirely equal to him, and still loves her to this day with everything he has.

Which brings me to my second point… respect for women. For you to claim that "no one has more respect for women" than yourself, is completely laughable. Your labeling of women as "fat pig[s]," "piece[s] of ass," and "eating machines," is beyond disgusting. And the fact that you sincerely believe your fame gives you the free will and right to sexually assault individuals is absolutely terrifying.

I distinctly remember being an 11-year-old in the car with my father when Britney Spears' "Slave 4 U" came on the radio. My awkward, middle-school self was singing along when suddenly he turned the song down.

"Don't you ever be a slave to any man," were his exact words to me, as he drove down the street to drop me off at swim practice.

At that time I was completely mortified, and just wanted to catch the end of the song so that I could mouth, *"Like that,"* and pretend I was on the stage at the 2001 MTV VMAs dancing with a python, but instead I was stuck listening to my father lecture me about the importance of self-respect. Today, I can't thank my father enough for that awkward moment. He raised my sister and me to always think for ourselves, to stand up and speak for what's right, no matter how uncomfortable it may be to do so, to never succumb to the constant peer pressure of "fitting in," and to always, always, always have respect for ourselves. Things that, by your track record Mr. Trump, you aren't the best leading example for.

Your past public statement to a woman about how good she would look "dropping to [her] knees," not only makes me angry for my own gender, but also makes me sad for all of the women in your life. What about your wife? Daughters? Grandchildren that look to you for guidance? Is this what you want them to take away at the end of the day? That it's okay to kiss someone without their consent? To rate them by the size of their chest? To tear down their self-esteem for the simple fact they don't fit into a size XS dress?

I've struggled with body issues for the majority of my life. I've never once been a size 0, had perfectly straight teeth, or a glowing complexion. And I can honestly say that after 25 years, I'm finally okay with it, and part of this self-acceptance I owe to my father. Since day one, he taught me the importance of knowing that someone isn't defined by a number on the scale, a chipped tooth (shout out to a Bud Light Lime bottle in college for that one), or the pimple on your chin. Instead, he's always stressed the importance of respect, honesty, and kindness...three characteristics in which you seem to be seriously lacking.

There are a lot of reasons why I have so much love and respect for my father but I believe helping my mother raise two girls into women is why I love him the most. There was never a sport I couldn't play or a dream I couldn't have, without knowing he would be there for me every step of the way. My father always has provided me with a feeling of security, and has always supported me on whatever path in life I choose to take, regardless of the fact that we don't always see eye to eye....a secure feeling that I believe you're very much incapable of providing to our country if elected as our next President of the United States.

Mr. Trump, I ask you to look around this country and tell me what you see. Black, White, Hispanic, Middle Eastern, gay, straight, bisexual, queer, rich, poor...our country is made up of so many unique individuals.

People that need to know, what my father has always taught me, that they have the same rights as any other person. Immigrants that need not fear of being sent back to the country they left in search of a better life in this one. Women that work the same job as men, only to fight for gender equality and still be paid 80% of what the opposite sex makes. **We need to know that the next leader of our country, will wholeheartedly fight for every single one of us, every single step of the way.** At the end of the day, I understand that the position of the leader of our country stems deeper than race and gender (and the fact that I think my father is the coolest guy in the world), but these two elements just so happen to make me who I am today, and I wouldn't change a damn thing about them.

Oh, and one more thing if you didn't know this already….I'm with That Nasty Woman.

46

As A Queer And Jewish Woman, Here's Why I Refuse To Be Silent About The Election Results

Tali Rainess

As a Queer and Jewish identifying woman, I am overwhelmed with fear and anger at the result of this election. I am baffled with the results that have divided our nation, and although I am saddened by this divide, **I refuse to cooperate with those who are in support of what Donald Trump stands for: pure hatred and the destruction of human rights.**

I am angry, and I accept this feeling as valid and well-founded.

Do not dare to claim my anger as invalid, unacceptable, and/or unwarranted. I am angry and I refuse to back down or subdue this anger in order to keep the peace.

I will not sit back and watch this nation be powered by this profound hatred. We are supposed to be the land of the free and the home of the brave and instead we have become a place that people are afraid to live in, pitied by countries everywhere. I am horrified at what has happened thus far with Donald Trump being the next president. Swastikas are being found, threatening my safety as a Jew. The statement "Fuck Fags" has been spread around threatening my safety as a queer individual. Assaults have happened to women in America as well.

I feel unsafe and I feel terrified.

So what do we do at this point? We stand strong and fight for what we believe in. Do not excuse the behavior of Donald Trump and his followers. This is not a matter of opinion or disagreement. This is our human rights being threatened. I stand by this and will not back down when questioned or intimidated.

I am angry, but that doesn't mean I am violent. I will not stoop to that level. I will act on my anger with love and a passion for justice. I encourage you to do the same. Violence and more hatred will not resolve our issues, but only make them worse.

As for many issues, silence and inaction are the deadliest on our end here. We must stay grounded in our beliefs. We must speak up and act on these beliefs. Hate will not win, love is more powerful. We have gotten too far as a nation to let this election destroy us. I will not give up, but I need you to not give up with me. I'm calling on you to honor the existence of minorities all across the country and fight with us. No one can do this alone.

For Trump supporters, if you don't understand why I am angry, please hear me out with an open-mind. This man has threatened to put up a wall. This man is against marriage equality. This man has mocked the disabled. This man has rape accusations against him. I want you to comprehend and take this in.

He is dangerous and America has given him power.

Where does that put us minorities then? It puts us in a state of uncertainty and threatens us. For those who refuse to understand this, I want you to know that we are here and we are here to stay. We are going to be loud and proud. If you have a problem with that, then so be it, but we are not backing down.

For my allies who are at a loss of hope, know that you are not alone. Trump may have won the electoral vote but the popular vote went to Hillary. You have many people on your side, fighting for their rights. Don't give up without a fight. We will prevail but it will take effort, strength, and resiliency.

Love trumps hate and conquers all. Keep believing and keep loving. That's how we will prevail.

47

We Must Be Upset But Never Fearful

Megan Melnyk

We have nothing to fear but fear itself. As I look upon those words proclaimed by FDR, during his first inaugural address, two conflicting feelings rise inside of me. The first is one of dismissal, rising from a feeling of disgust towards a man who was just elected the President of the United States. *How can these words hold any weight against a campaign that has promised the exclusion of the rights of Americans?* The second, however, is hope.

Donald Trump's campaign was founded on fear. It preyed on the anxieties of Americans who were hurting and worried about the condition and safety of our country. It took advantage of those disparities and gave them names: illegal immigrants and Muslims. It took advantage of the fear of having a dishonest president elected and turned "Anyone but Her" supporters into Trump supporters. And now that this campaign of fear has officially been successful, it has instilled fear into the ones that it targeted.

And fear has run rampant.

I have listened to the unguarded terror of friends who are scared that their rights will be taken away. I have read the shock and dread that people express over the trajectory of our nation on social media. I have felt the sorrow of my friends as I hold them. And more than anything, I have seen it in the faces of people all over my school campus: a dejection like no other.

However, amongst the terror, is hope.

I listen to friends who vow that they will stand with those who have been made targets. I read the declarations of people who will support the communities who have been made victims through Trump's campaign. I can feel the support of my friends as they hold me. And more than anything, I see it in the signs that my classmates wear around campus that say "I will support you."

We cannot fear. This nation is not governed by solely one man, it is governed by the people. It is governed by a people who right now are shouting that we will not allow our brothers and sisters to be targets; we will stand with them.

It is governed by a multitude of people who are not happy with the policies that have been put forth by the man elected. Even a proportion of the voters who supported Trump could not say they voted for him with pride, but rather out of fear, and will not support the policies that he will try to enact.

We cannot fear, for fear is what has caused this mess.

Instead, we must have hope and love and support for one another. As one of my friends put it, love trumps all. In our heartbrokenness, we must stand together and heal together and prepare to face what is ahead of us. Fear is not the end of this. Donald Trump is not the end of this. Terror has not won. As former President Obama stated, "The sun will rise in the morning." So I will be upset over the election, but I will not fear its results.

Conclusion

Very soon, perhaps by the time you read this, President-elect Trump will be President Trump. He will enter office with one of the lowest approval ratings of a new President in recorded history, and he will be dodged by accusations of fraud, sexual assault, and unethical business practices.

But he will be our President.

As the United States and the world works to navigate this unorthodox Presidency, Thought Catalog will remain a platform for your thoughts, expressions, fears, and jubilations. And no matter what happens, or how long it lasts, we will be here to continue cataloging the improbable and impressive political journey of Donald Trump.